Fun & Games & Higher Education

Fun & Games
& Higher Education
The Lonely Crowd Revisited

Randle W. Nelsen

Between the Lines
Toronto

Fun & Games & Higher Education

© 2007 by Randle W. Nelsen

First published in 2007 by
Between the Lines
720 Bathurst Street, Suite #404
Toronto, Ontario   M5S 2R4
Canada
1-800-718-7201
www.btlbooks.com

All rights reserved. No part of this publication may be photocopied, reproduced, stored in a retrieval system, or transmitted in any form or by any means, electronic, mechanical, recording, or otherwise, without the written permission of Between the Lines, or (for photocopying in Canada only) Access Copyright, 1 Yonge Street, Suite 1900, Toronto, Ontario, M5E 1E5.

Every reasonable effort has been made to identify copyright holders. Between the Lines would be pleased to have any errors or omissions brought to its attention.

   Excerpts from End Zone, by Don DeLillo, copyright © 1972 by Don DeLillo: used by permission of Viking Penguin, a division of Penguin Group (USA) Inc.

   Excerpts from "Remembering Reuel Denney: Sociology as Cultural Studies," by Randle W. Nelsen, originally published in The American Sociologist 34, 4 (Winter 2003), 25-39: reprinted with kind permission of Springer Science and Business Media.

   Cover images: front upper ©iStockphoto.com/Belinda É. Stojanovic; front lower and back ©iStockphoto.com/Sandra Henderson

Library and Archives Canada Cataloguing in Publication

Nelsen, Randle W.
        Fun & games & higher education : the lonely crowd revisited / Randle W. Nelsen.
Includes bibliographical references and index.
ISBN 978-1-897071-31-1

1. Play – Social aspects – United States. 2. Recreation – Social aspects – United States. 3. Education, Higher – Social aspects – United States. I. Title. II. Title: Fun and games and higher education.
GV14.45.N44 2007   306.4'81   C2007-903436-5

Cover design by Jennifer Tiberio
Text design and page preparation by Steve Izma
Printed in Canada

Between the Lines gratefully acknowledges assistance for its publishing activities from the Canada Council for the Arts, the Ontario Arts Council, the Government of Ontario through the Ontario Book Publishers Tax Credit program and through the Ontario Book Initiative, and the Government of Canada through the Book Publishing Industry Development Program.

Contents

Acknowledgements   vii

Introduction   1

Chapter 1 • **"The Party's the Thing"**   5

Chapter 2 • **Cultural Studies**   19
The Sociology of Reuel Denney

Chapter 3 • **The Party Hits the Road**   41
A Ticket to Ride

Chapter 4 • **Big Games**   57
"The Decline of Lyric Sport"

Chapter 5 • **Tailgating**   71
"A Feast of Strangers"

Chapter 6 • **The Fourth Quarter**   97
Higher Education Joins the Party

Chapter 7 • **Overtime**   115
Distance Education, Sociability,
and the Song of the Sirens

Notes   133

Bibliography   141

Index   148

Acknowledgements

I AM WELL AWARE THAT SCHOLARSHIP, as I have argued in this book, is a social activity; hence the length of these acknowledgements. I do apologize if I have left anyone out who should have been included, and I thank you.

First and foremost, I express my deepest gratitude to my superb editor, Robert Clarke. This book as it now appears is not only different but also much improved from the draft manuscript he first saw. His organizational and writing skills (plus his good-natured ways of poking and prodding me out of complacency and into revisions and additions) have been literally transformative. Rob's enthusiastic encouragement of this project was unflagging, and I cannot thank him enough for fitting me into his busy schedule.

Another key player has been my secretary, Karen Woychyshyn. As usual, she delivered in the clutch with unfailing good humour. Karen typed the initial draft and much subsequent revision, and also – as one might expect from a friend – offered sustaining good cheer when the work got me down. Thank you.

Four colleagues deserve special mention. My long-time pal David Peerla offered his usual sage advice, research skills, and acumen. Give David a question or a problem and he will find an answer. His curiosity and research scholarship are infectious and freely given as a friend. My friend and colleague Lisa Korteweg also proved most willing to exchange ideas and participant observation strategies with me. Her take on my observations and interpretations reveals a questioning mind that continues to illuminate. Similarly, Norene Pupo of York University, a friend and former student of mine at McMaster, has used her lively and critical mind to engage with my work for the past thirty-five years. Gary Genosko provided important bibliographic input and encouraged my renewed interest in popular culture. I thank him for giving me an opportunity to publish some of my early thinking with regard to the subject matter of this book.

I also want to thank long-time Lakehead colleague David A. Nock and Lawrence T. Nichols, editor of *The American Sociologist*, for their scholarly interest and advice. In addition, three other colleagues and former students of mine, Steve Bosanac, Walid Chahal, and Brian McMillan, have been generous and enthusiastic in their continuing support of my work.

This book took shape around the ideas found in the scholarship of Reuel Denney, who was my mentor more than forty years ago. Although it has now been a dozen years since he died, his thinking and diverse interests continue to provide intellectual stimulation and inspiration. Another Denney admirer and fellow graduate student from the 1960s whose friendship continues, Bin-ky Tan, along with his partner, Ruth Tan, encouraged me to re-examine Denney's work. I am grateful for this suggestion and the Tans's support; the result was a rekindling of some popular culture interests from our University of Hawaii days and Reuel's classes.

I want to extend a big thank you to the staff and editorial collective of Between the Lines for their support and vision in being able to see the worthiness of the arguments presented here. Special thanks go to Paul Eprile and Steve Izma for their high-quality hard work and encouragement. It has been a pleasure working with you. I also received a warm and hospitable welcome from the staff at the Rauner Special Collections Library of Dartmouth College, where I worked with the Denney archives.

Finally, I want to recognize and thank both my extended and immediate family.

My cousin David Hanson, a University of Oregon Ph.D. who provided valuable insights concerning this research, and his partner, Susan Hanson, made my field trip to an Oregon Duck football game possible. It was great fun hanging out with them, and the childhood memories, laughter, good food (side trip to winery and beach included), and fellowship generously offered made this research trip a blast. My second family and long-time friends Charlie DeFalco and Diane Stevens and their children offered the usual warm support I have come to count on over the years. My daughters, Emilie and Rebecca, provided insight into many of the matters discussed herein. I especially want to thank Rebecca, seemingly headed into the "family business" of sociology, for her scholarly interest and exchanges regarding my ideas, and for rounding up and sharing some of her university friends in aid of my research.

Most important of all, I thank my partner of a quarter-century, Carol Ann Collins. She is a sustaining force in all I do. During the preparation of this book she was there for all the ups and downs that a writer-researcher goes through. She and her family, the Montreal clan, made the field trip to Dartmouth College memorable. Above all else, Carol Ann, as a principled and fun-loving feminist, offers me a daily role model to emulate and measure myself against. She is also the best storyteller I know, one who can always make me laugh. Thanks for everything, Carol Ann.

Introduction

FOR ME, WRITING THIS BOOK HAS BEEN A LABOUR OF LOVE, the culmination of a desire to bring together my long-standing interests in higher education and popular culture in a manner that appeals not only to academics but also to other interested readers. I have been either a university student or a professor since I was eighteen years old – forty-six years now and counting – and this lifelong preoccupation with academic life has been a roller-coaster ride of stimulation and boredom. I must confess that more often than not I have found the writing of professional academics to be obtuse and tedious. Some early readers of this manuscript found it a bit too breezy or journalistic in style: code, perhaps, for being too accessible and not academic enough. Other readers pronounced it thought-provoking.

Some readers have been critical of my tendency to make arguments that tie together what they see as disparate, or fragmented, themes. I welcome this apparent criticism as another strength of the book. Indeed, seemingly disparate themes and trends come together in a university setting and in what is written about it. The current popularity of higher education (with its spiralling enrolments), the increasingly variegated mix of students from different cultural and class backgrounds, the ever-broadening age-range of students, the increasing multiplicity of special programs, area studies, and interdisciplinary projects: all of this seems on a surface level to be the institutional embodiment of disparity and heterogeneity.

Seen at another and deeper level through the lens of cultural studies, though, today's universities have become homogenized by and are responding to the dictates of a popular culture dominated by televised mass sports and "reality" spectacles, video-gaming, and a YouTubed Internet. My central argument is that higher education has become edutainment at the expense of scholarship. A party atmosphere has become ever more prevalent – extending from the tailgate party in the stadium parking lot to the classroom.

Homogeneity in higher education is an effect, an outcome, of how larger socio-economic arrangements and the popular culture, along with subcultures, work together to shape the institution of formal schooling. That is why I find it instructive to revisit the work of sociologist Reuel Denney on the subcultures of football and hot-rodding and his writings on the conformist anxiety of the lonely crowd in their search for sociability. Tracing the history of both a corporative automobility and college football as they became part of the entertainment industry permits me to examine the intersections of work, education, and play as they are reshaped over time by corporate business and economic interests. The institution of higher education is an ideal place to examine these intersections because in the process of being certified university students are a key to the reproduction of basic societal institutions and values, as well as of the marginalities of oppressed groups. Socialization to the main drift of popular culture's present moment results in a process of centralization, which contributes in turn to both the increased homogenization of societal institutions and increased conformity among individuals.

The anxious search for sociability and community is, of course, part of the human condition. After all, we are social animals. The lonely crowd's historical journey from the 1950s to the present reveals the outlines of today's culture of fun and its business orientation. It was fun, and therefore an excellent research gig, to attend tailgate and homecoming parties and the Big Game, but the most important consequence for me as a social analyst is that through my participant observation I am able to share with readers a first-hand account of what I studied. This book tells how a tailgate party fills a void, making the lonely crowd less lonely. It tells how corporate growth is based upon a generational class-consciousness and a search for community togetherness that reconstructs socio-economic arrangements without disturbing the status quo. My focus on universities, sports, and partying, then, is something more than just an interesting way of discussing changes in post-secondary education; it is also an analytical comment on the kind of society and culture developing in both the United States and Canada.

Returning to the criticism that the book contains annoyingly disparate themes, I do admit to raising, in the final two chapters, a number of higher education issues that are not fully explored. I hope this is thought-provoking, and if so I'll be happy to plead guilty as charged. The contentious issues and troubling questions plaguing the academy and its place in the outside world have been written about at length and are all too familiar to university participants. A partial list includes: the connections between the politics of diversity and identity, and the impact of special access programs on admission equity; the ways in which marginalized groups help to refocus and realign academic opportunity and program creativity; the place of research alongside teaching; the manner in which corporate and state funding sources intersect with and undermine university autonomy; the role of state-funded universities in serving the interests of the public at large rather than the private interests of the wealthy; the connections between student plagiarism and grade inflation and the emphasis upon graduate school education; the increase in tuition rates in relation to the increasing percentage of students working full-time and part-time; the connections between academic excellence and both traditional and more recent views of scholarship; the factors of accountability, which should be considered by an academy that is being transformed into a consumer marketplace; the role of technology in reinventing research skills and determining learning (teaching and research) agendas – training and vocational professionalism versus education and personal growth as academic priorities. The argument I develop herein speaks to and should be useful in understanding at least the final four issues on this list, but I also hope that it has even wider applicability.

In today's higher education, both student and faculty "consumers" are moulded in a manner that emulates the edutainment culture of the mass media. Pacification is the order of the day, while critical thinking and resistance all too often take a back seat. Fun culture takes over, and the university as a result is undergoing serious and, in my view, undesirable alterations.

If Reuel Denney were still around to observe the changes that have brought us to the university of today, I think he would be supportive of my lament. Towards the end of his career he supplemented his long-standing interest in youth culture with writings directly focused upon developments and trends in contemporary higher education. In what was often an understated manner he offered resistance to the deficiencies of formal education in schools, raising questions and providing critiques. I am doing the same because, like Reuel, I have spent most of my life inside the university and I care about what goes on there.

Indeed, if we want to have any chance of structuring a higher learning, a scholarship, capable of questioning and countering the less than challenging conformity and pull of popular culture, then provocation and resistance are not luxuries; rather, they are necessities.

CHAPTER 1
"The Party's the Thing"

> The realism and the fantasy of the audio-visual media never can and never will exhaust the play impulse . . . and we know that many people in many ways seek less vicarious uses of leisure time. The impulse toward sports is one of these ways, even though an individual who is a spectator rather than a participant may find his vicarious thrills in the game the other fellow plays. – Denney, *The Astonished Muse*, p.97

"PARTY ON WAYNE!"

"Party on Garth!"

These signature lines from the 1992 hit *Wayne's World* represent an experience – a "lifestyle" – that goes far beyond the movie theatre and the *Saturday Night Live* television skit that gave birth to the film. In the years since Wayne (Canadian comedian Mike Myers) and his buddy Garth (Dana Carvey) brought these lines to life on the big screen, the party has moved out of Wayne's basement, the setting for the duo's zany, and fictitious, cable-TV show – so far out indeed that the "party on" line has become a suitable tag line for today's corporate-dominated and orchestrated world at large. It remains a particularly apt formation in any consideration of young people and popular folkways and the realm of higher education.

The famous rebellious youth experience of the 1960s to early 1970s was also, at least partly, about having fun. As writers Joseph Heath and Andrew Potter put it in their book *The Rebel Sell*, the counterculture of the 1960s saw having fun "as the ultimate subversive act."[1] The hippies,

Heath and Potter say, transformed hedonism "into a revolutionary doctrine." From Heath and Potter's point of view, for those youth it was all about how the dominant society achieves order through the repression of the individual, "at the expense of promoting widespread unhappiness, alienation and neurosis," whereas "pleasure is inherently anarchic, unruly, wild." The logical response "must therefore lie in reclaiming our capacity for spontaneous pleasure – through polymorphous perversity, or performance art, or modern primitivism, or mind-expanding drugs, or whatever else turns your crank."

It turned out, though, that in the end some of this was not all that much fun – the drug-inflicted deaths and the infamous Rolling Stones Altamont concert being the most obvious examples. And while partying might be fun, it is not subversive, as at least some members of the counterculture might have imagined. Even when a few guys get together and decide to follow (literally) the Beastie Boys lyric "You gotta fight for your right to party," the resulting actions will more often than not tend to be commodified and co-opted to serve existing socio-economic arrangements – as the counterculture also soon found out.

The urge to party and to view partying as, if not revolutionary, at least an integral part of rebellion has been around for a good while. The Boston Tea Party of 1773 – the climactic American Revolution event of resistance to British attempts of direct taxation – was, of course, a very serious event, but perhaps it is an exception that helps to back up the generalization that the sociability of partying is not usually revolutionary. The glorious history of "partying hard" and "party animals" is nothing new – it goes back, at the very least, to the hedonist movement of the ancients Greeks and, later, the Roman Saturnalia – but, as in those cases, it usually has very little to do with overthrowing the state. The 1920s party that was the Jazz Age fed off prevailing capitalist arrangements. Charleston-dancing flappers and others revelling at speakeasies celebrated an economic boom that produced newly minted fortunes for hundreds of thousands of investors. Sandwiched between the end of the Great War and the beginning of the Great Depression, the Black Tuesday stock-market crash of 1929, which ended the "roaring twenties," shook prevailing arrangements without breaking them.

Girls, and everyone else, it seems, just wanna have fun. "If I can't dance, I don't want to be part of your revolution," is a quotation (often seen on T-shirts) attributed to Emma Goldman. But she didn't really say that, exactly. Rather, what the famous anarchist did was become furious at the "impudent interference" of "a young boy" who once remarked to her at a party that her "untiring" dancing, her "frivolity," would only "hurt the Cause" – "It did not behoove an agitator to dance." Goldman told him to mind his own business. "I want freedom, the right to self-expression, everybody's right to beautiful, radiant things," she told the boy.[2]

For Goldman, those things were what anarchism meant, and she said that she would live in that way "in spite of the whole world – prisons, persecution, everything. Yes, even in spite of the condemnation of my own closest comrades I would live my beautiful ideal."[3] To party, especially in the face of adversity, is to make a powerful cultural statement. Yet the principle also works in notably different ways. Take, for example, Mardi Gras 2006 in New Orleans, held only six months after Hurricane Katrina devastated the city. At the time of the festival two thousand people were still unaccounted for ("missing"), and thousands were without shelter, water, and other necessities. A raging controversy over whether or not even to hold a Mardi Gras celebration was added to charges of general corruption, misappropriations of funds, and a dereliction of duty on the part of government officials at all levels. In the final analysis the urge to celebrate and keep alive the party tradition (and perhaps, at the same time, the tourist industry) won out. Amidst all the death and destruction, the levelling of New Orleans, the city set aside two million dollars a day *not* to restore water service or build much-needed shelter, but to host the 2006 edition of Mardi Gras.

For me, one of the most distinctive and telling examples of this general cultural phenomenon of Americans (and Canadians) at play is *tailgating* – and I don't mean tailgating in the sense of that all too familiar practice of driving so closely behind another vehicle that you become an accident waiting to happen. I mean tailgating in another established sense – the one defined in a dictionary as "Designating or pertaining to an informal meal served from the open tailgate of a parked car."[4] This brief and sanitized dictionary explanation, however, omits an important meaning: that this informal meal is also a festive celebration that not only permits family and friends to enjoy food, drink, and each other's company but also offers them an opportunity to meet strangers and enlarge the circle of friendship that lies beyond kith and kin. Not surprisingly, the dictionary definition also omits any reference to the big business, in the billions of dollars, that tailgating has become.

In autumn at campuses across the United States, Saturday's "Big Games" bring the car and football, gridlock and gridiron, together in this popular cultural practice known as the tailgate party. Here the car becomes not only the warm-up for radio's and television's play-by-play coverage but also kitchen, bar, music centre, and so on – literally the centre of the party. In its transformation this use of the ubiquitous road vehicle is transformative, an extension of the stadium to the parking lot and in some ways a levelling, a sort of democratic counterpoint, to the difference between the box seats on the fifty-yard line and the cheap seats in "the nosebleed section." This practice, this "feast of strangers," as it has been called, brings together passions that are close to the hearts of most North Americans: our keen interest in food and competitive sports, and our continuing love affair with the automobile. One writer traces the practice of tailgating back to Harvard and Yale universities in the early twentieth century, opining that in the annals of American society it is "an inevitable byproduct of the Industrial Revolution (which begat both the carburetor and the turkey frank)."[5] Charles R. Frederick, Jr., a folklorist at the University of Indiana, argues that Americans "connect vehicular travel and food in ways that are peculiarly American." He adds:

> Our landscape is dotted with "fast food" restaurants made all the more convenient by "drive-up" windows. We eat behind the wheel as a matter of course. . . . The typical tailgating experience relies on the automobile, not simply as a mode of transportation but the vehicle tailgate itself, or trunk, must serve as the groaning board that holds the food, drink, and service integral to the event. . . . Each vehicle provides a spatial reference point for the activity around it. Celebrants tend to stay close by their stocks of food and drink which are openly displayed. During the colder months, late in the season, a charcoal grill often provides a warm focal point for the tailgaters.[6]

The tailgating party, like the promise of the open road, is an opportunity to celebrate personal freedom in a personalized do-it-yourself manner; and the love affair with speedy and sexy vehicles of all sorts in turn led to such things as the growth of roadside lodging and, in America, the Interstate highway system. The car has played a central role in transforming, while at the same time reinforcing, basic institutions and values. But tailgating is also fascinating to me because it is so closely related not just to what is called "automobility" – <u>an expression of autonomous individuality</u>, of self-determination – but also to other American phenomena: <u>football,</u> and sport and entertainment in general. <u>Tailgate parties are not just festive occasions, but business.</u> The practice calls up the intersection of play with work, class, and the business culture – even, as we shall see, the realm of higher education.

Tailgating is also of great interest to me because it harkens back to the work of a former professor of mine, Reuel Denney. This man, variously thought of and labelled as a humanities, English, or American studies professor – he was also a celebrated poet – is infrequently remembered by sociologists as a lesser-known collaborator, the other being Nathan Glazer, with David Riesman in the writing of *The Lonely Crowd: A Study of the Changing American Character* (1950). This book became the best-selling sociological classic of all time, with over one million copies sold from its publication in 1950 to 1971 and close to a million and a half through 1995,[7] the year Denney died. The book's triumvirate of tradition-directed, inner-directed, and other-directed types continue to provide inspiration for many analysts and are so well known they have become almost clichéd.

Yet neither Denney's role in the publication of *The Lonely Crowd* (the publisher's choice for a title) nor a large amount of later work made his name a household word in the social sciences, and his work continues to go largely unrecognized by sociologists. Perhaps this is simply due to the passage of time. After all, more than fifty years have passed since the publication of *Lonely Crowd,* and fifty years since the University of Chicago Press first published what I consider Denney's most lasting contribution to sociology, his marvellous extended commentary on American popular culture, *The Astonished Muse* (1957). Denney's catholicity of diverse interests, his globalness, might also have something to do with hiding his sociological contributions. His work crossed many of the traditional academic boundaries, which means that it has never been singled out, claimed, and promoted by any particular discipline. During a fourteen-year affiliation with the University of Chicago, Denney was never made an official member of its sociology department. That he spent his later years and most of his career in Hawaii, away from the U.S. mainland's centre stage, may also be an important contributing factor to his relative obscurity. (And Hawaii, incidentally, is where I caught up with him.)

I would argue that Reuel Denney's work has had a major influence upon the development of sociology for more than half a century. It is an influence that continues, and as is the case with work that moves towards "the classic," there is a certain timelessness about it. That Denney's analysis of popular culture in the United States in the middle of the twentieth century might continue to serve as a valuable guide in understanding the twenty-first is a judgment affirmed by the University of Chicago Press in approving republication of *The Astonished Muse* in a new thirtieth anniversary edition in 1988. Likewise I believe that the thinking of this pioneering figure should not go unappreciated or be lost to the generations that follow.

Denney's large body of work as a social analyst took in cultural studies of Americans at play, including writings on the subcultures of football and hot-rodding, and work on television and the electronic media, advertising and architecture. It seems to me that in his writing and thought we have what I think of as a "Denney postmodern." Of course, this is a postmodern that does not feature women or analysis grounded in the work of feminists – Denney was primarily socialized, and much of his most important writing was completed, prior to the rise of second-wave feminism in the 1960s. (I have accordingly refrained in my citations of his work from linguistic and other "revisionism" that would replace his use of "the generic" male pronouns and words like "mankind" with today's universally accepted use of gender-neutral language.) Still, the sociological analysis found in his writings anticipated much of what is being discussed in the classrooms and lecture halls of today – what we now call "cultural studies," that is, sociology as cultural studies – before it became fashionable.

One of Denney's major themes – and of great interest to me in this book – has to do with obstacles to autonomy in work and play, especially among the middle classes. For instance, in *The Astonished Muse*,

Denney expands upon the work of his University of Chicago student Gene Balsley (1950) in analyzing the post–World War II subculture of hot-rodders, seeing this do-it-yourself movement – with their supreme interest in ornaments, chrome, tailfins, wire hubcaps, and the like – as a case study of "participative purists," part of his exploration of outsider-insider relations, the strange and the familiar.[8] Hot-rodding, he writes, is "an activity which involves a wide range of economic groups, which hooks into the major daily consumption patterns of the nation, and which has had a powerful amateur influence on the professionals in its own field."[9] But the study is not just an investigation of a subculture – of what Denney, in a delightful and telling phrase, referred to as "a salon of the refused"[10] – but also an examination of major consumption patterns in the United States. In the same book he puts this kind of cultural experience into the framework of a curious shift occurring in American society, a shift that had to do with the use of leisure time. "Do we use leisure or does leisure use us?" he asked in one article.[11] In *The Astonished Muse* he suggested:

> The time that is made available for leisure in the new suburbs tends to be used, perhaps temporarily, not only for specifically social rather than individually leisureful purposes, but also as a time in which the productive impulses not fully satisfied at work can be discharged.
>
> One of the results is a shift in the relations among the spectatorial, participative, and more individualized forms of leisure choice and among the market decisions and personal activities of which each is composed.[12]

Following Denney, then, I would at least in part view tailgating – and to some extent experiments with cars and football – as the Lonely Crowd's quest for community and togetherness. With the three character types introduced in *The Lonely Crowd* – tradition-directed, inner-directed, other-directed – Riesman, Denney, and Glazer were suggesting that individual character and behaviour were shaped and directed by the different feelings and orientations predominant in each case – shame (tradition), guilt (inner), and anxiety (other). In the book the authors reflected upon the dominant character or ethos typically produced in different societies, arguing, for instance, that in Western society "inner direction" was prevalent in the late-nineteenth and early twentieth centuries, and that "other direction" had become more prevalent in recent years. They contended that Americans in 1950 were quickly moving from moral and "Father Knows Best" guides for behaving properly to a kind of nervous anxiety about acceptance that was cuing and governing social interaction. To explain this change they used as an analogy the difference between a gyroscope and a radar screen. A gyroscope, a spinning wheel on an axis, keeps a plane or a ship on course, pointing out direction by means of resisting change in its orientation. A radar screen constantly and continually scans the environment (the horizon) to detect the presence and direction of various objects (which will need to be avoided).

The stock Englishman posted to a far-flung corner of the Empire who dons formal attire for tea in a steamy African jungle because this is what you do at 4 P.M., no matter where you are, is a tradition-oriented, inner-directed person. The Organization Man looking for clues and direction as to how to win friends and influence people, how to fit in, wherever he is – cocktail or tailgate party, the office, football game, neighbourhood garage sale, and so on – is other-directed.

The other-directed individual is anxious. High anxiety and concerns about acceptance in ambiguous and new social situations become commonplace, a part of daily routine in today's postmodern society, and sociability is heavily freighted with symbolism. What (where, when) you eat and drink, how you arrange your sexual life, and how much of that life is public knowledge, whether you are popular or friendly and with whom, and a host of other everyday/everynight activities and concerns all fall under increasingly intense scrutiny.

For the other-directed individual who is "at home everywhere and nowhere" at the same time, the crowd is lonely. The party – to party on – eases the burden, making the crowd somewhat less lonely and perhaps, for the individual, even providing a start in carving out a less lonely, less crowded subcultural niche. Standardized curriculums with neatly tied up packages of learning to be mastered and graduated also make the crowd less lonely and reduce anxiety – as do the university's logo and mascot on the T-shirt or sweatshirt worn to the football game, and all kinds or manner of consumption – the right pair of "brand-name" jeans, a familiarity with and love of popular songs, and buying and playing video games, for instance.

Denney saw sports history as "a social process, parallelling change in the rest of the society, the rise of industrialism, the softening of puritanism, the needs of war, and the process of ethnic assimilation."[13] Adding to that approach, I would argue that marginalized groups (African-Americans, women, the poor) have not been entirely included in the freeway party – the promise of freedom offered by automobility has not been wholly delivered. The autonomous individuality expressed in automobility, it turns out, is not about democratic community, but about market-driven consumer capitalism. It turns out that the capitalism that hypes both automobility and the do-it-yourself movement as "new frontiers" is simply a new frontier for economic expansion and more corporate concentration. It is expansion powerful enough to co-opt the hot-rodding subculture, "the salon of the refused," as well as the other-directed individual's search to find a unique place of specialness in the Lonely Crowd. Rebellion, again, becomes capitalist commodification and co-optation, and whether it is the Big Three automakers or another industry or business, centralization leads to homogeneity and conformity. As Denney puts it in his article "American Youth Today" (1962), "Within the great internal market of the nation, the automobile, the electronic wave, and a variety of other forces have served as equalitarian tropism by making young people richer than they have ever been, and rather more like each other than they have been since the Civil War."[14]

American football as a kind of democratization in the world of entertainment is part of, and subsumed by, a larger theme central to Denney's sociology: the battle of capitalism and its attendant, standardized professionalism as it intersects with democracy; and the game's original emphasis upon a less-regulated, craft-based discipline grounded in amateurism. In his case study of football in *The Astonished Muse* Denney speaks of changes in that game as "the decline of lyric sport" – a theme I use to guide my thoughts on the subject. Football – and here I am considering in particular the development of the American college game – has grown into a large profitable business attracting big corporate sponsorship, and in the process it has travelled down a professionalized road that takes it far away from its amateur roots. One result is a troubling re-emphasis of cultural violence and militarization that encourages us to objectify players and each other. Key rule changes differentiate the U.S. brand of football from its soccer and rugby antecedents, and two groups of off-field specialists, technologists and sportswriters, have played a key role in the transformation of the sport. These groups continue to be instrumental in creating an organizationally efficient and scientific football that forms the basis for a sociable occasion.

Sportswriters as a group were and are singularly important, and they helped to create a national audience for the American college game. They interpreted football as a social event, infusing the game with meaning that went well beyond its similarity with the country's industrial folkways. Their narrative structure and observations penned a party, a spectacle, grounded on the sociability of sport as entertainment. The stage was set for creating a new social context that would merge the interests of Knute Rockne and Henry Ford, the game of football and automobility – as Denney put it, Knute Rockne was the game's Henry Ford – which brings us back to tailgating. Indeed, the very sociability of the tailgate party, both its reinforcement of class solidarity and its potential for class mobility, is promoted by three interwoven football narratives that together form the core of the tailgate business – the search for community togetherness, corporate growth, and class-consciousness – narratives that make the Lonely Crowd less lonely. The tailgate party, as part of an entertainment industry that reproduces socio-economic arrangements, fills a void. It provides a fun-filled opportunity for do-it-yourself direction and hopeful expectation to millions of Americans, students among them, without disturbing the status quo.

The sociability surrounding college sports also has an integral connection to, and effect on, the classroom side of the big business that we know as higher education. The university is both a place and an experience. Increasingly the experience is becoming a search for sociability, an attempt to counter inadequate opportunities for a satisfying informal public life and the isolation that this inadequacy sustains and re-creates. Today's higher education emphasizes the sociability of the party and a consumerist lifestyle that often combines shopping, alcohol, gaming, computer play, and television spectacles at the expense of a different kind of sociability, grounded on reading and writing about ideas of substance, that, at its best, characterizes scholarship. Universities, as James B. Twitchell puts it, "are really in the business of retailing an interesting new product – the emotional credential – to consumers who have been taught to shop around."[15]

Corporate branding is part of this phenomenon: it advertises the variety to be found among the "emotional credentials" retailed by universities. The differentiation inherent in this variety not only divides the market but also melds with intercollegiate sports and tailgate partying. These days market branding has become seen as a necessary, indeed crucial, tool in a university administration's quest to secure and sustain the financial health of the institution. It would appear that student attachment to a particular – a unique – brand makes even more crowded lecture halls less lonely and offers a chance for individuals to stand apart from the crowd. Again, not only is the party scene central to this branding, but the sociability found at the party also helps to recreate social class relations. At the same time, too, it helps to create an increasingly homogenized and professionalized sameness among the student body.[16]

Another facet of this same theme appears in how the technology behind "distance education" helps to put students in a mould where they turn out to be very much like one another. Denney himself made an excursion into an early form of distance education (see chapter 7). Today's education at a distance relies heavily on packaging knowledge (knowledge packages) for "delivery" to students in a manner that not only creates conformity-addicted students but also promotes and reproduces the standardization and homogeneity of the larger socio-economic order that structures today's higher education. The electronic management of distance education also promotes an increasing inability to invest worth in a place and thus intensifies the search for sociability. Computers are used not only to decontextualize learning but also to pacify student and faculty "consumers" of "learning packages," connecting them to market-dictated teaching and research. The connections between technologically mediated education at a distance and the party as a lifestyle revolve around (or lead us back to) *The Lonely Crowd*'s category of other-direction and the adoption of conformity to relieve anxiety. In brief, McLearning removes the anxiety of knowledge tangents – the semi-organized/ reorganizing confusion of scholarship/creative thinking – in favour of the security of conforming to a (technologically) standardized curriculum.

For me, the writings on education of both Denney and his contemporary Marshall McLuhan provide inspiration in this regard. Knowledge creation and communication are social activities, a type of sociability – a point that connects Denney's writings with some of the interests of the German sociologist Georg Simmel as set out in his classic work on sociability.

Placing Denney in the tradition of Simmel and alongside McLuhan not only contributes to a critique of distance education but also helps me to carry forward my themes regarding the general character of today's higher education. Essentially my argument is that the nature of the university as a sociable place of higher learning is undergoing a fundamental change. Increasingly the university can be found in front of a keyboard and screen at any computer terminal anywhere. Education at a distance diminishes the university as a place of scholarly experience. Nowadays, too, what is promoted on campus is a self-help, pop-psychology type of sociability grounded in a growing array of consumer activities – with the emphasis above all on fun. Speaking of a different brand of consumer activity in 1958, Denney pointed out:

> I should like to say that in connection with whether the American consumer is or has been a slave or a rebel, that I think that in some of his purchases of certain commodities and services now he's neither one nor the other quite, he's mostly what I would call an indentured servant, that is he serves out his time with a certain kind of car, a purchase of a new kind of house and so on.[17]

A prime example of this youthful consumerism and the workings of Denney's "play impulse" was on display across Canada and the United States in autumn 2006 as intense gamers camped out all night, some for two nights, to be the first new owners of Sony's PlayStation3.[18] The Associated Press reported fisticuffs, beatings, stabbings, and shootings from Massachusetts, Connecticut, and Pennsylvania in the East to Ohio, Kentucky, and Virginia in the Midwest and South to California on the West Coast. The Canadian Press reported little violence among Canadians, who, true to their cultural socialization, exhibited more orderly, less chaotic behaviour than did their U.S. neighbours. Canadian outlets hired overnight staff to ward off trouble and ensure safety, set up an xbox 360 for campers to play while they waited, offered free food and beverages, and handed out numbered tickets to ensure order and fair treatment. In Edmonton a distributor held a lottery, guaranteeing ten eager gamers that their wait in below-freezing temperatures would result in ps3 ownership. Supplies were limited, with no more than 40,000 units available in Canada in this initial offering, and gamers were desperate to both play and profit as the new game's first owners. Several campers, university students among them, reported plans to make their patience-in-line pay off by advertising their Can.$650 purchase on ebay to potential buyers who would help them turn a tidy profit of some $3,000.

"Party on Wayne!"
"Party on Garth!"
"Excellent!"

CHAPTER 2

Cultural Studies

The Sociology of Reuel Denney

> The integrity of the symbol system derived from sports is largely a function of two things. First, sports recruitment draws on habits built up in the imaginative generosity of childhood and youth.... Second, sports recruitment is a big business with a market to satisfy.... These two characteristics of the sports world must surely go far to explain why sports, like entertainment, are usually ahead of churches and schools, for example, in responding sensitively to the moral pressure for freedom and equality in our society. Thus in the segregation issue, for instance, sports and some kinds of popular entertainment have established community between the races before other social institutions could or would.
>
> – Denney, *The Astonished Muse*, pp.98–99

IT WAS IN HAWAII IN EARLY SEPTEMBER 1965, in a classroom close to the University of Hawaii's East-West Center, that I first encountered Professor Reuel Denney.

By the end of our first meeting in what we referred to as "the sociability seminar," my graduate colleagues and I were all thoroughly impressed with the breadth of our new teacher's interests and his list of reading requirements and suggestions. It was a list designed to make us think about our own socialization and cultural circumstances in relation to others.

We read August B. Hollingshead's *Elmtown's Youth: The Impact of Social Classes on Adolescents* (1949) to learn about the impact of differing social classes on the youth of a small midwestern town in the United States. We continued our measurement and discussion of social class differences in the United States by reading two other mid-twentieth-century classics, W. Lloyd Warner's *Social Class in America: A Manual of Procedure for the Measurement of Social Status* (1949) and Russell Lynes's *The Tastemakers* (1949).[1] When we read two of Denney's favourites, Sir Harold Nicolson, *Good Behaviour: Being a Study of Certain Types of Civility* (1960), and Francis L.K. Hsu, *Clan, Caste and Club: A Comparative Study of Chinese, Hindu, and American Ways of Life* (1963), we found ourselves being exposed to both a British and a Hindu-Chinese view of the structural interaction of social classes and several other matters of cultural import. We also read J.A. Pitt-Rivers, *The People of the Sierra* (1961), a detailed description of the social structure of a rural community in southern Spain.

During a winter 1966 seminar on "mass communication," which was team-taught by Denney and Floyd W. Matson, we read Matson, *The Broken Image: Man, Science and Society* (1964), a book that caused us to reflect on social studies and the humanities in relation to "science," along with Marshall McLuhan's then-new and now infamous *Understanding Media: The Extensions of Man* (1965), and Denney's own recently published, groundbreaking tour of American popular culture, *The Astonished Muse* (1964). I recall that Denney was extremely humble, even shy, about assigning his own writings. He often needed a prompt from Matson and senior students to discuss his own work in greater detail.

Of course, in the classroom we also discussed *The Lonely Crowd*. Because we were his students, and fond of him, my colleagues and I at times would speculate as to which of the character types (tradition-, inner-, or other-directed) Denney was most fixed on developing in our own group. The betting money and general consensus were on the other-directed, but I always put in a good word for the inner.

In addition to *The Lonely Crowd*, our seminars made reference to both Alexis de Tocqueville and his time-honoured study *Democracy in America* (1835 and 1840) and Thorstein Veblen's studies of the leisure class and business enterprise (1899 and 1904) – writers whom we were encouraged to read. Then there were two important mid-century books, Oscar Handlin's *The Uprooted: The Epic Story of the Great Migra-*

tions *That Made the American People* (1951), and Eric Hoffer's recounting in *The True Believer: Thoughts on the Nature of Mass Movements* (1951) of what happened to many of these same immigrants in the mass social movements that accompanied their arrival. Hannah Arendt's now well-known view of *The Human Condition* (1958) and the new *Structural Anthropology* of the French social analyst Claude Lévi-Strauss (1963) also served as suggested reading. Finally, we read a large number of reprints from the Bobbs-Merrill series. A few authored by Georg Simmel were especially important, because Denney was particularly interested in what this German sociologist had to say about dyads, triads, and small-group interaction in general. He also was particularly fascinated by Simmel's work on the symbolism to be found in mealtime manners and rituals.

In retrospect, it is clear to me now that the books Denney had us read and the issues we discussed as graduate students in the 1960s grew from and were strongly tied to both his own early life experiences and his work as a developing social analyst. Formal schooling played a role, but I judge it (based in part on his autobiographical remarks) to be in large part supplementary. The connection between Denney's early life experiences and his sociological work as a student of culture can be seen in his writings on the subcultures of football and hot-rodding as well as his interests in the communication possibilities of the mass media and architecture, and the intersection of work with play in business culture.

"The Child Is Father to the Man": Early Life Experiences and Sociology

Reuel Denney was born in 1913 into a family with strong ties to New England, New York City, and Ireland. His father, Reuel Salano, was the only male child of a Maine doctor who died when his son was only seven. Denney's grandmother remarried, to a New York engineer-inventor, Harmer Denney, co-inventor of the Denney price-tag-making machine. Denney lovingly remembers his father, a sales manager of office equipment, for his success in business, but most of all for "his ethos of family devotion. He taught me to play all my sports except skiing and was gentle and empathic with me in my crises of growth – and my alterations at such times between wordy revolt and silent sulking."[2]

Denney gives credit to his mother, Katherine, for his love of and facility with languages and for much of his sociability. Katherine was the daughter of Irish immigrants. Her mother had earned her passage to the United States by working as a "dairy maid" in Ireland (in Clomel on the River Suir in Waterford), while his grandfather Nicholas, known as "Big Nick," was training in a nearby district (Tipperary) "as the master of coach-teams for a large English-owned estate." After landing at Ellis Island, Denney's grandmother secured what turned out to be a good position when "she was taken on as a front parlour maid by the Brokaws of Locust Valley, Long Island, the parents of the future groom of Claire Booth (Brokaw) Luce."[3] Nicholas complemented her good fortune by landing well-paid, secure employment with the New York City Fire Department. In brief, Denney's maternal grandparents lived (from Ireland to New York City and from the barn to the front parlour) both ethnicity and social class, and they knew the problems and potentials associated with each.

They also knew and loved books. They loved the pleasures of reading and storytelling. Denney fondly recalls his grandmother willingly fulfilling his requests for the retelling of a favourite bedtime story called "Johnny Magory," a cautionary nineteenth-century Irish parable that, according to Denney, allowed him to contrast warm family acceptance of his virtues with the bad boy faults of Johnny and his punishments. He also remembered how his grandfather spent his retirement imagining life as a country squire while reading and rereading a few favourite novels secured from the Brooklyn Public Library. All of this shaped Denney's early childhood. He grew up in Brooklyn "in a household addicted to both storytelling and to reading."[4]

The Brooklyn neighbourhood of Bensonhurst, where Denney spent his early years, was bursting with immigrant and first-generation Germans, Irish, Italians, and Jews. It was here that Reuel first became a student of words, of language and languages. As an adult he was able to read Latin, Italian, Spanish, Portuguese, French, "a good amount" of Greek, " and a fair amount of German and Sanskrit."[5] He also had a passing familiarity with Yiddish and Japanese. It was a linguistic journey with a global breadth that connected him first with the ancient civilizations of Europe and then with those of Asia. The legacy of his early years on "the punch ball streets of Brooklyn" would be a life-long love and fascination for the sociability occasioned by the spoken and written word – and its legacy would hold him in good stead in his employment-related mobility through Buffalo and Chicago and across the Pacific Ocean to Honolulu's East-West Center.

In his eighth year, 1921, Denney's family moved west to Buffalo, but he continued his connections with his old neighbourhood, spending summers at his grandmother's house in Brooklyn. His street education in ethnic differences continued, and this learning was supplemented with an early exposure to history and popular culture courtesy of his "accessible" Uncle John, a firefighter who once went into a burning mansion and rescued "a great pile of the publications *Life*, *Judge*, and *Puck* for the years 1880 to 1900."[6] Denney spent many rainy days with this collection, in the process developing a great love for cartoons, comics, and magazines.

In Buffalo the Denneys took up residence on a street just beyond the outer limits of that city's wealthiest district, Central Park. It was a neighbourhood conducive to a continuing education in social-class differences and sociability:

> My life as a school-boy and high school student in this neighborhood was on a scale of comfort, assurance, and even social luxury that seemed to justify the portrait of the affluent United States represented in the *Saturday Evening Post* of the time. All the good fathers of the neighborhood drove a car and our landlord's wife drove one of her own, a La Salle. My grammar school friends recruited me as a guest golfer at the Park Club, a demesne only a few miles away, where we ran up tabs for soft drinks and apple pie with ice cream. Even our Boy Scout troop was a sort of Cadillac of its kind, with its own clubhouse in a marvelous deserted commuter railway station and privileges at a country camp called Toad Hollow. No one in this neighborhood except teenage boys drove a Ford Model T. It should be no shock that during these years I accepted all this almost unconditional prosperity and security as my due.

In Buffalo, then, Denney got his first taste of the meaning of "leisure" for people of a certain high station in life, and he would later expand upon these early experiences through his abiding interest in leisure, voluntary associations, and play. He moved between Brooklyn and Buffalo and Sunday dinners at the Niagara Inn, where the owner, a family friend – a combination of "Rathskeller man and Chaucer's Tabard Inn-master" – sequestered the family in "a special dining room of privilege set apart from the open dining area of the ordinary customers."[7]

In this early life the roots of his interest in subcultural and leisure differences as parts of "the process of social levelling-down" were firmly implanted. In Brooklyn and in Buffalo, and later in Hanover, New Hampshire, as a student at Dartmouth College, Denney would become attuned to the levelling potential of democracy as it connects to the power of association – the power of the collectivity played out against the American ideological backdrop of "rugged individualism." He lived the angst of juggling and balancing the guilt of inner-direction with the anxiety of other-direction.

Denney writes about how, in fall 1925, at the age of twelve, "in the very middle of the Jazz Age," he and his friends donned Plus Fours ("a kind of economy-size knickers popularized by, among others, the golfing Prince of Wales") and "set out on a long walk to Main Street and Bennett High School."[8] At Bennett, Denney recalls "no lemons" among the faculty assigned to him, and it was here that he read Milton and was introduced to the poetry of Keats, whom he describes as "the Cézanne of Romanticism," with a modern counterpart to be found in the early Rilke.[9] He also found himself joining a school literary society and participating in public-speaking classes. Outside school he travelled a slightly different path, playing sandlot football and baseball, while also finding time for the more upscale game of tennis. In the long run all of this implied that the relationship between the social and the intellectual – a kind of sociability, if you like – might be worthy of exploration. Above all, his experiences in Buffalo implanted a particular kind of faith in social democracy:

> All you needed was clean cars, ears, and fingernails and the capacity to observe the simpler rules of etiquette. I learned to play golf badly – as a guest player at the Park Club. My father joined the Buffalo Athletic Club during the prosperities of the 1920s and I joined the Saturday morning table there, a group of kids signing checks for pop-overs after the swimming class. The fact that at the end of grammar school many of these

people were sent off to private school, Park, Nichols, The Seminary, or even distant and improbable institutions such as Andover, was merely an event in class aspiration. The social democracy was real.[10]

In June 1928, at only fifteen years of age, Denney graduated from high school feeling well served by "the loyally classical curriculum of my courses at Bennett and the skill of the teachers who taught them."[11] He entered Dartmouth in the fall, but even before that, in the summer, he learned more about social class and the ways of the wealthy on Wall Street, where he was employed as an office boy (and at other times as a runner delivering stocks) at the investment firm of Spencer Trask and Company. Here he learned the social hierarchy and office politics of a high finance bureaucracy and got to know his way around New York's financial district. He also picked up "a firm grounding in the reference materials (*Moody's*, *New York Times*, *Consolidated Railway Guide*, *The Steamer Guide*, and *The Social Register*) employed by the Research departments and all the magnates of the district."[12] Later this knowledge would be invaluable as he fashioned insightful financial stories (on the Bretton Woods Conference, Bethlehem Steel's wartime shipbuilding, and Giannini's Bank of America) for Henry Luce's *Fortune* magazine in the mid-1940s.

Denney's high-school and university years (1925–32) were marked by patterns that were hard to ignore. Chief among these were a notable anti-Catholicism, which led to Democrat and anti-Prohibitionist Al Smith's defeat in the election of 1928, and a kind of continuing and recharged religious fanaticism resulting from the anti-Darwinism of the Scopes Monkey Trial of 1925. These kinds of events featured what Denney described as "menacing behavior from crackpots, many if not all of them from lower middle-class backgrounds, who formed hate-Smith and even KKK affiliations in the neighborhood."[13] Finally, a further entrenchment of class divisions was reinforced, deepened, and solidified by the Crash of October 1929 and the subsequent Great Depression of the 1930s. These developments and others made Denney a good deal less sanguine and more realistic about social democracy in the United States. Still, he continued to enjoy sports favoured by the leisured upper classes, adding sailing to tennis and skiing as one of the three passions that would remain all his life. Visits to the Adirondack woods and the history of that region in upstate New York were two other passions that marked his youth.

Denney's great interests in identifying trees and in visual art had begun in his youth with walks through various city parks supplemented by Boy Scout camp visits to the Adirondacks in the summers of 1925 through 1927. It had been a chance encounter in the Adirondacks with a Dartmouth student employed as a counsellor at a neighbouring camp that figured most prominently in his decision to attend that school. Denney and others from his camp were mightily impressed by John Scott's "combination of woodsmanlike appearance and scholarly background" and struck by the fierce pride he exhibited in praising the college he was attending. Denney decided "on the spot" that he wanted to go to Dartmouth over his father's preference for Harvard.[14] So, in the fall of 1928, he set off from the old New York Central Station in Buffalo: "I carried into the Pullman with me a suitcase, a portable typewriter, a tennis racket, a set of golf clubs, a pair of skis, and an easel. The steam locomotive speeded up its puffs, jerked the long train to a start, and I was on my way to the school famous for its love of the outdoors."

Denney reports little about his Dartmouth years with the high-water-mark exception of making a first acquaintance with English professor Sidney Cox, a friend to poet Robert Frost. Cox became a mentor and long-time friend – Denney would dedicate *The Astonished Muse*: "In memory of Sunday evenings with Sidney and Alice Cox." Graduating in 1932, at the age of nineteen, Denney decided against graduate school as a hedge against the declining economy. "I had run through my father's generosity to the amount of the $5,000 that it had cost him to send me to Dartmouth." He decided that he "ought now to put in time in the school of hard knocks, away from the ivory tower."[15]

Returning to Spencer Trask as a regular employee late in 1932, Denney left the following spring and joined a college classmate and friend, Charles Mayo, "who was sailing his yaul to Florida." A year later he returned to his hometown of Buffalo, where he supported himself doing "dead-end jobs" while writing "verse and prose."[16]

One of his jobs in the mid-1930s was at the Buffalo factory where the Houdaille Shock Absorber Corporation manufactured its famous automobile part. As the payroll chief's "functionary," he collected and calculated employee time cards and continued to be educated in ethnic relations and the divisions and dynamics of social class. "The main lesson of this experience was that the Anglo- and German-American middle managers regarded the Polish men on the machines as their social inferiors: the salaryman over the piecework wage earner. The Western over the Eastern European."[17]

The influence of both the factory job and his next employment – as a high-school English teacher in Buffalo from 1936 to 1941 – would lead him to think about the possibilities of a socialist alternative to the capitalism of the ailing U.S. economy. At the high school he became involved with the teachers' union and edited a local union periodical. He also recruited and coached prize-winning debate teams noted for the so-called "Oxford style" playfulness of their debating demeanor. In his classroom he employed innovative pedagogy in motivating a group of so-called "slow learners" from households where English usage was weak, in effect teaching a version of what would be known today as an English as a Second Language (ESL) class.

In the mid-1930s, shortly after he started teaching, Denney met what he called "the two most important persons" in his life.[18] The first, Ruth Lois Norton, he met at a party given by his Buffalo childhood friend, the painter William Rowe. Ruth and Reuel were married in a civil ceremony on July 1, 1938, and would be partners for life. Denney credits Ruth for much of his mental well-being and happiness, and speaks with pride of her many accomplishments.

The second most important person appeared at a dinner party in late 1936 or early 1937. David Riesman, then a young law professor at the University of Buffalo, and Denney hit it off immediately. Before the evening was over they had already arranged a tennis match, the first of thousands they would play with each other. It was the beginning of what Denney describes as a life-long friendship and scholarly collaboration:

> In the course of time, I became very much impressed by the insights of Riesman into topics that we were both interested in: resistance to Fascism and Nazism, the threat of reactionary voices, such as that of Father Coughlin, in American life – the general themes of American culture such as Puritanism and Romanticism. I was a little surprised to meet a law

professor and wife who read heavily in modernist literature (especially Joyce and Kafka) and I believe he was a bit surprised to meet a secondary school teacher of English and debate coach who read Tocqueville. These common interests became a basis of a friendship that continued in Vermont beginning in 1941 and in New York beginning in 1943 – and extended itself to the University of Chicago, beginning in 1947. There I taught with Riesman and collaborated with him and Nathan Glazer in writing *The Lonely Crowd*.[19]

Denney left high-school teaching and Buffalo in 1941, the year that his and Ruth's only child, Randall, was born. Behind him was a first book of poems, *The Connecticut River*, published in 1939. Ahead of him was a 1941–42 Guggenheim Fellowship spent writing in Middletown, Vermont. He also did a stint with a new organization called the Volunteer Land Corps, a "major prototype of the Peace Corps," finding city youth wartime summer farm jobs. Denney had a rather distasteful brush with the editorial Republicanism of *Time* magazine, serving as a writer-reviewer, followed by a "promotion" to *Fortune*, where he achieved a certain notoriety for his stories on the 1944 world financial conference at Bretton Woods and on the California banker A.P. Giannini. The Giannini story on the huge Bank of America became a source of argument and editorial conflict between Denney and his more conservative *Fortune* editors. It was time to look for a new paycheck.

Denney's search for employment resulted in a job with the staff in English and Humanities at the College of the University of Chicago. Having been sponsored and encouraged by Riesman, he was now ready to join him, taking up duties in fall 1947. Denney remained at Chicago until 1961 (with trips during the 1950s to Colorado and Cambridge, Massachusetts, to direct seminar classes at the Aspen Institute and at Henry Kissinger's international seminar at Harvard) and then moved on to finish his career at the University of Hawaii in the Department of American Studies and with the East-West Center. At the East-West Center he became devoted to understanding the relations between Japan and the United States as well as helping to revive Hawaiian Studies so that the indigenous people of the islands he loved could have more opportunity to tell their own stories in their own way.

Cultural Studies of Americans at Play: A Sampler

One of the things from his childhood that Denney brought forward to us as his graduate students was his keen interest in the socializing and other-directed effect of the comics as a storytelling medium. Denney loved to watch and interact with his "accessible uncle" John, who, for the amusement and edification of extended family and friends, used themes in comic strips to explore similar themes in daily life. "My uncle saw the city through the comic strip, and he saw the comic strip through his sense of the city."[20] For Denney as well the comics were always more than simply "an escape" from the round of everyday activities. They provided serious comment on the developing "lifestyles" of the United States at the midpoint of the twentieth century – comments on changing attitudes concerning ambition, acquisition (the consumer culture), work, play, and the connections among these. As Denney's graduate students we became conversant with the theme of escape and its attendant ambiguities often found in "other-direction."

The complexity of other-direction has to do with intersections between "taste cultures," "taste-makers," and social classes.[21] In the new consumer society, a society of acquisition, leisure pursuits begin to replace work in creating an identity – in answering the question, "Who am I?" High anxiety becomes commonplace, a "normal" part of our lives, and symbolism plays a large part in everyday sociability. Eating and drinking habits, the organization of sexual and family life, friendships and leisure-time activities, the mode of transportation for the commute to work: all of these and many other aspects of our usual routines and tendencies carry symbolic messages and come under close observation.

Denney knew these tendencies or conditions as lived experience. His own youth spent crossing class lines provided not only a test of his "inner-direction" but also an education in observing how others sell a particular self, a subculture, and the larger dominant culture. He analyzed the "magic" of advertising, moving deftly between the media's pitchers (the production team) and its catchers (the variegated audience) to show how mass culture tried to standardize even "the-do-it-yourselfer," the "self-sold consumer."[22] Advertising not only sends us on a search to find and recover our identity, but is also entertainment.

For Denney, advertising joins the games it promotes as part of sports history as "a social process," and I recall seminar discussions of hot-rodders and do-it-yourselfers and of the professionalization of football and tennis as popular entertainment. Analyzing the first Coca-Cola advertisement of 1905, which "showed a young man with golf clubs and a young lady with a tennis racket," Denney connected the ad to changes in the games and to the class position being represented. The ads "must have made tennis players out of some young men and women who would not otherwise, even at the urging of the women's magazines in the first decade of the century, have learned to cry 'Love,' to the delight of kids at the fence."[23] Coca-Cola also helped to oversee the transformation of golf from a "dude game" that Theodore Roosevelt advised Taft to avoid[24] to a White House style of life characterizing the Eisenhower administration.

Play becomes a new high priority in consumer society as factories and businesses encourage and sometimes force employees to mix work and play (the executive golfing foursome, the business lunch or dinner, the company picnic, the corporate box seat). *Having to work at play* – a sense of leisure that becomes increasingly standardized by capitalist markets – was a major theme that became intensely familiar to Denney's students – and it was the subject of his prize-winning *Harvard Business Review* article on "The Leisure Society," in which he raises his major concern in the subtitle: "do we use leisure or does leisure use us?" This theme, as it plays out and is structured in economic markets, is also found in his written work on hot-rodders and footballers.

In *The Astonished Muse* Denney shows how hot-rodding redrew the line between participants and spectators as amateur hobbyists began to have an increasingly difficult time knowing whether they were in the game for fun or for business. In its original form hot-rodding represented a deviation from the main technological drift of Detroit's Big Three automakers. On the production side, according to Denney, it served not only as amateur criticism but also as a creative impulse to the Detroit professionals. But "perhaps hot-rodders are most influential where they try out features that would otherwise be years slower in acceptance. From that point of view, the usefulness of the hot-rodder to Detroit lies more in the field of consumption pioneering than in technological advance."[25] The hot-rodders, who "unmistakably constituted a salon of the refused" in the beginning, were being transformed into the mass-society spectators of Veblen's "vicarious we."

Denney discusses that "vicarious we" not only along the less to more active continuum of spectatorship but also along a continuum of pleasure in work that both contrasts and mixes with most Americans' ideal of pure pleasure. Change in the mid-twentieth century involved an increasingly fuzzy line dividing leisure from work, a shift in relations involving forms of leisure choice and market decisions.[26] For instance, the advertiser, he wrote, "becomes, at the extreme, a documentarist of the social scene, as interested in telling people what they are culturally entitled to buy as he is in whether they have the cash for it or in his own products as a candidate for the purchase."[27] He argued that the effect of the advertisers' messages "is to provide redefinitions of personality and culture in which are blended information, publicity, and entertainment. . . . Only time can tell whether the profession will succeed in modeling itself on Lorenzo de Medici or on P.T. Barnum."[28]

Turning to footballers and their game, Denney explained the speedy development as well as the early and quick acceptance by Americans of their variant of English rugby as a consequence of the new game's close fit with "other aspects of their industrial folkways." He analyzed and described football as a game that was becoming increasingly rationalized around the turn of the nineteenth century: "The mid-field dramatization of line against line, the recurrent starting and stopping of field action around the timed snapping of a ball, the trend to a formalized division of labor between the backfield and line, above all, perhaps, the increasingly precise synchronization of men in motion."[29] Efficient synchronization of a formalized labour force combined with the introduction of new rules – the new manners governing play – helped to take local proclivities and local colour, and inequities, out of the game. The result was movement towards a professionalized standardization and a business-oriented centralization of the sport.

In one article, published in 1951, Riesman and Denney provided a history of Knute Rockne's game as it developed into an American cultural staple. The authors outline how the tenth- and eleventh-century English game became formalized in the United States as both entertainment and big business. They show how "the ambiguities" of the English versions of football/soccer (the kicking game) and rugby (the running game) were melded into Rockne's version – how Ellis of Rugby's 1823 faux pas of picking up the ball and running with it became a "mistake turned into innovation" as Americans added the forward pass and downs with minimum yardage gain and offside rules to create a more exciting, quicker-paced game. Football's U.S. version revealed much about the character of American culture – not only the Americans' taste for the excitement of action-driven entertainment but also a desire for the no-nonsense standardization and centralization of business favoured by their rule-bound, legalistic approach.

American football's transformation into big and profitable entertainment also revealed "an element of class identification." The authors note that early football in Britain was played by an elite or upper stratum before lower-strata audiences who were at least as much interested in carefully observing the players to be sure they demonstrated the "good form" of "gentlemen" as they were in keeping track of the score. The American experience and game were different, played by a collegiate elite, but watched by audiences who, having had some experience in playing the game, "were unwilling to subordinate themselves to a collegiate aristocracy."[30]

Denney was especially insightful on the question of how differences between amateurism and professionalism are related to social class. He perceptively analyzed the often lower-class youth amateurism of hot-rodder culture as threatening to the middle-class professionalism and respectability of the Detroit automakers who sought to normalize and standardize the amateurs. "Not a few people seemed to feel, without quite saying so, that the duty of young Americans was to buy cars, not to rebuild them. To rebuild a car, it appeared, was an attack on the American way."[31] Put another way, and to incorporate a 1990s advertising pitch, to mess around or tinker with the Chevy in the backyard was to mess with capitalism, "the heartbeat of America."

Buying and not tinkering with the Detroit model pits corporate restraint against the tendency towards individual freedom. That democracy as freedom for both individual and community might be engendered by upward social mobility (that is, the purchase of a new factory-built car) was another concern raised in our classes. We soon learned to look beyond the automobile or the material good itself to share Denney's awareness that cultural capital walked hand in hand with monetary capital and was often the advance guard for crossing class, gender, and ethnic barriers.

Denney taught his students to become attuned to social transformations such as the advent of the tailgate party in the university stadium parking lot – the historical changes in cultural meanings attributed to material artifacts. His work is replete with models to be emulated in this regard. For example, in sketching the history of the car as both democratic possibility and media extension Denney writes: "Sometime between 1920 and 1945, roughly, the auto had passed through a stage of its existence symbolized by the comic strip 'Gasoline Alley.' As auto, it had lost much of its old novelty as transportation; in order to retain glamor it had to become, in differentiated forms, a kind of daily apparel."[32] As this beautifully constructed metaphor reminds us, we as a culture have been changed by the auto, and as changed beings we do our best to make our own modifications, pushing the boundaries of the medium as both message and massage.

Messages sent and received across different media is a theme that Denney shared with Canadian media guru Marshall McLuhan (1911–80). Denney's cultural studies anticipated, rather than simply incorporated, McLuhan's, and while Denney did not experience McLuhan's popularity the work of the two men had much in common,[33] and they knew it. McLuhan was aware of Denney's analyses of popular culture, and his citation of Denney's car-as-daily apparel observation is a case in point.[34] They not only read each other (Denney read and appreciated *Understanding Media* and, earlier, *The Mechanical Bride*, while McLuhan did the same with *The Lonely Crowd* and *The Astonished Muse*), but also shared an engagement with the writings of de Tocqueville, Veblen, T.S. Eliot, and Ezra Pound.[35]

As both teachers of English and artists, Denney and McLuhan understood media as translators. Denney understood that Americans in the 1950s were in the process of exchanging the "hot" medium of radio for the "cool" medium of television, and his emphasis on comics as a cultural window agreed with McLuhan's assessment that comics were the "*Mad* vestibule to TV."[36] Both scholars concentrated on communication forms (media) and how they intersected and altered the unity of business and leisure in popular culture. They focused on how one media form, say, radio or comics, changes and merges into another, say television, and how these transformations not only alter us as individuals but also alter the popular culture that we both create and serve. They shared a keen interest in the speeded-up dialectic of decentralization and integration that characterizes the electronic process, while maintaining an awareness that any medium tends to amputate the function that it extends. Thus, while television in a manner of speaking gives us the globe as extended neighbourhood or village, in so doing it limits our ability to experience our own residential neighbourhood as a village. Television telescopes our view, but it both extends and narrows our vision in the same moment.

The reality that we humans create and use media so as to extend ourselves, extend the power of our human faculties, is a theme that Denney returned to regularly. This basic insight is often at the bottom of his expressed interest in democracy – specifically, the democratic and communal possibilities of cars, football, and television as both entertainment and big business – and, interestingly too, he also applied this insight to architecture.

Denney's interest in architecture involved studying the ways in which buildings can speak to us, and he became especially engaged in looking at the connection between architecture (buildings as extensions of our skin) and democratic possibility. His work speaks to the meaning of space and time in the architecture of different eras and cultures, to the connections between work and play, to fundamental ideas in democratic states, and to a more specific point that he was fond of reiterating – namely, that buildings and their locations serve the functions of communication and display as well as production.

He makes this point beautifully in "The Suppliant Skyscrapers," a chapter in *The Astonished Muse*. Here he discusses corporate buildings that make use of large glass surfaces, such as Lever House, New York's first glass curtain-wall skyscraper (1952) and the Manufacturers' Trust Company building on Fifth Avenue (1951–54), showing how the architectural capture of light illumines "the business totem pole." He asks, "In a central Manhattan building, who could doubt that the photons that fall on this or that desk are significant in terms of occupational status?" The person "nearer the light" is the person "higher up."[37]

Later, architects of the post-Depression era reversed the previous generation's emphasis favouring the elite's "second city" with its invisible (from below) "Hellenistic palaces, urns, and tombs of the earlier rooftops" by "dragging the gods of décor down from the topmost levels to the lowest levels of visual accessibility."[38] Vertical movement down and away from the top-floor, corner office was accomplished by a horizontal shift from the inside towards the outside of urban business buildings at street level. This "opening-out" at the lower levels made possible by advances in steel-frame construction carries a good deal of social meaning. Glass at street level acts not only as "a showcase for the advertisement of anyone who stands inside" but also as an invitation for the public outside (well-mannered and appropriately dressed, of course) to enter the private world of the business corporation. As Denney points out, this more inclusive skyscraper is an architectural triumph of public relations promoting and advertising the dominant ideology, as skyscrapers move from conquering colossi to democratic suppliants (today's version being patrolled by high-tech security firms).

The 1960s and Sociology: Revolutionary Prospects

For us as students, all of this too was happening during the 1960s, that decade that often seems to be summed up by the now infamous phrase, "sex, drugs, and rock'n'roll" along with Timothy Leary's dictum, "turn on, tune in, drop out." It was, in the popular mind, a time of the "sexual revolution" courtesy of The Pill, fuelled by "pot" and LSD to the accompaniment of the Beatles, Rolling Stones, Bob Dylan, Jimi Hendrix, Janis Joplin, the Doors, Grateful Dead, and the Jefferson Airplane – even, from Canada, the Guess Who, The Band, Neil Young. The Party was in full swing everywhere from San Francisco's Haight-Ashbury district, the universally acclaimed centre of "flower power," to Toronto's Yorkville area and Rochdale College.

The sixties were not, however, all about hippies and Woodstock. Many in my generation spent a good portion of their undergraduate and graduate days as I did, often in the library when not in class, staying under the radar of the authorities, and getting ready for a white-collar job that I for one hoped would turn into a career. In our study breaks in fraternity-house living rooms, in campus coffee shops, on the steps of the library, and outside our classrooms we discussed school-work and current events in the non-Hendrix "purple haze" provided by

Liggett and Meyers (King Size). Our discussion topics included JFK's youthful presidency and assassination, increasing militarization and the growing anti-Vietnam War movement, the civil rights movement and the radical activism of the "black-power"-inspired Black Panthers, as well as the key issues and thinkers in the burgeoning women's liberation movement, as it was then called. Many of us participated in these major social movements of the day, which were often centred on university campuses.

In addition to Vietnam teach-ins and protest demonstrations on virtually every campus in the United States and Canada, there was the University of California at Berkeley's "free speech movement," the student protest and takeover of the administrative offices at New York's Columbia University, the occupation by "black-power" advocates of buildings at Cornell University in the state of New York, and the University of Michigan-based Students for a Democratic Society and their Port Huron statement of democratic ideals and defiance. All of these preceded the well-publicized 1970 National Guard murders/killing of four students during an anti-war protest at Ohio's Kent State University.[39]

Canada also had its own well-documented protests – at Simon Fraser University in British Columbia, Quebec's Sir George Williams University (now Concordia) in Montreal, Toronto's York University, and the University of Toronto, to name a few.[40] By 1968 students in North America were joined by those in Europe in protest movements across the Western(ized) world.

The student activism of university social protest movements constitutes the other half of the campus party during the 1960s. These movements were the precursors of and are the models for the political organization and protest found in today's demonstrations focusing on environmental issues (global warming and forest clear-cutting) and corporate globalization and branding, and, lately, against the wars being waged by the United States and its allies (including Canada) in Iraq and Afghanistan.

Sociology as a discipline was and is part of all this. During the 1960s sociologists joined the struggles against militarization, corporatization, classism, racism, and sexism. The discipline developed to include both "radical," "action," and "feminist" sociologists who left the positivism of "objective" sociology behind and were up front about disclosing both their political agendas and biographical information – a subjectivity that put them in touch with the "touchy-feely" counterculture(s) of the times.

Some of us, while supporting the new directions of sociology at the time, were less optimistic about sociology and its revolutionary prospects. We viewed its practice in university and corporate settings as supporting and reproducing the status quo. I remain among the doubters of sociology as revolutionary practice, but unlike Heath and Potter, in their *Rebel Sell*, I do think the protests and demonstrations of the countercultural 1960s, while eventually co-opted, were progressive in moving both the United States and Canada at least a little way towards the political left. These countercultural activities were not simply occasions to party. Rather, they were for the most part serious attempts to change the status quo, and sometimes they eventually succeeded – the American withdrawal from Vietnam and various victories for women's rights are cases in point. And yet, the various sixties movements and protests often did involve good times. A definite party/festival-type atmosphere prevailed, and a critic could not go far wrong in suggesting that the participant observation of 1960s sociologists in the cultural events characterizing that decade marked the beginning of a transformation of parts of the discipline of sociology to what we know of today as cultural studies.

Denney's Postmodern: Creating and Interpreting "the Social"

I believe that in both seminars during the 1965–66 academic year Denney guided us as students by outlining and characterizing a version of the postmodern, though I suspect most of us were not very aware of what we were doing, and none of us at that time, of course, would have characterized our activity in that manner.

In what I think of as Denney's postmodern, media are all-encompassing environments, and they play a major role in creating and manipulating marginally differentiated audiences and markets.[41] Media as sociability are a big part of our struggles to find and sustain (recover) our identities both as individuals and as a culture. Advertising as a kind of pseudo-sociability is best viewed as the business of entertainment with the aim of "educating" mass audiences to the so-called benefits of buying different lifestyles. Recognition of both difference and similarity, then, is key in this new, media-created relativity of time and space; all knowledge is provisional and points to an ever-changing representation as boundaries are continually made and remade. The knowledges of many audiences are subjugated by the power and authority of mass media and mass communication, and the promise of democracy demands in the interest of fairness (justice) and the well-being of all that their voices be heard.

Well before Pierre Bourdieu and a host of postmodern theorists popularized the concept, Denney understood that the society evolving under late capitalism (whether we label it postmodern, global, post-global, or even modern) is mostly about differences in "cultural capital."[42] Most importantly, he knew that a good way of understanding the significance of different kinds and amounts of cultural capital, and their relation to one another, was to study popular culture. As a result he raised questions and suggested answers that could contribute to a growing understanding of what makes life meaningful in our daily round of routine activities. At the centre of his work he investigated and emphasized the importance of how humans create and interpret "the social" – how they make meaning out of the dialectic of reconstruction and deconstruction.

Denney's many inquiries and concerns ranged well beyond my brief outline here. But in essence, then, they include his interests in urban spaces and the sociability to be found there; in mass communication and architecture as an expressive, artistic medium; in mass media and the power of advertising; in the connections between work and play, and the obstacles to autonomy they share; in the role of the market economy in structuring leisure and the reverse; in identity as it is continually reformed by the intersection of individual character and cultural context; in subcultures as part of identity formation and a window into the dominant culture; in cultural standards as they are disciplined by both professionalism and amateurism; in the possibilities for both freedom and restraint found in democracy; and in the general study of popular culture and in popularizing scholarly work, an interest that characterizes the portfolios of those commonly referred to today as "public intellectuals." It is a list at the heart of sociology/cultural studies and one that continues to change, renew, motivate, and inspire this student.

Today's facile talk about role models, mentors, and mentoring doesn't quite catch the affable wisdom of Denney's Renaissance-like mind – a mind and manner that held myself and graduate colleagues enthralled, wishing that the seminars would not end and standing in line outside his office to get his take on our individual concerns and projects.

Denney gave his time with good-natured graciousness, and as one of my readers he took an interest in my master's thesis work at a time when I had little to say. His influence was so strong that several members of my graduating class of 1967 – including myself – considered staying on at Hawaii. A couple of the students did remain there to undertake doctoral work in American studies. I gave serious thought to this idea, but the press of family obligations together with the necessity for a larger paycheque than a graduate assistantship could provide sent me back to the mainland.

In retrospect I think we were drawn to Denney's inquisitiveness, his playful curiosity, and his openness. He treated us more like intellectual colleagues than graduate students, while playing down his own considerable accomplishments. I can remember an office visit when we both commiserated about what we were missing being at the campus on the island of Oahu, and he told me how he sometimes felt somewhat out of touch with and cut off from what was happening in the metropolitan centres of the mainland. When intellectual common ground was lacking – and from my end it often was – Professor Denney always found something we could share. As we talked he would be smiling, his eyes twinkling from behind the smoke of his ever-present cigarette (severe pneumonia in his seventy-fourth year finally forced him to quit the habit).

In our personal encounters with him we keenly felt his writer's capacity to, in his words, "familiarize the strange and to defamiliarize the accustomed."[43] Sometimes he was almost too self-effacing. You just had to like a guy who, when asked in an interview to give advice to aspiring writers, politely refused with these words: "Advice to aspiring writers I leave to those who have been able to make a living out of letters alone."[44] What graduate student in the mid-1960s or even today, embroiled in the expensive certification process of chasing a graduate degree, could not identify with Reuel Denney, B.A., who described his paid employment at Chicago and the talent that surrounded him there as "a kind of free graduate and post-graduate education" that he had received just by being on the premises.[45]

CHAPTER 3

The Party Hits the Road

A Ticket to Ride

DEMOCRACY IN PRACTICE rarely matches democracy in theory. The history of the American democratic experiment certainly teaches us that if equality of opportunity is a major democratic goal, it is not often achieved. It seems that some are always more equal than others. This has certainly been true for what American studies professor Cotton Seiler calls "the republic of drivers." Seiler argues that this abstract community of drivers and their assumed mobility and, thus, freedom, hide "the very real criteria for personhood" to be achieved in the republic: "generally, whiteness, maleness, and membership in the middle class."[1]

As with social mobility, automobility – physical movement through space and across geography – is limited by the usual barriers of class, gender, and ethnicity/colour. It is, then, embedded in the dialectics of a larger social system, playing a role both as part creator and part a creation of that system. In the final analysis autonomous individuality (freedom) as expressed in automobility turns out to be less about democratic community, a republic of drivers, and much more about market-driven consumer capitalism.

Automobile production, ownership, and travel have had a tremendous impact on the American landscape.[2] From the developing car culture emerged the tent houses and cabin camps of the 1920s, the tourist camps of the 1930s, and finally the motels of the post–World War II era that soon lined the newly built Interstate highway system. Of course, the nascent car culture led to more than simply roadside lodging. According to architecture and American studies professor Daniel I. Vieyra, "By the 1920s, the auto had become the lifeblood of the petroleum industry. Previously by-products of the refining process, auto oriented petroleum products like gasoline, motor oil, and lubricants accounted for 90% of the industry's production by the 1920s." The rubber industry (automotive tires, and trim elements), plate glass industry (windshields), and the steel, machine tool, and paint industries all benefited from the "quantum leaps" in demand that came with the car culture boom, and from the adoption of the mass-production techniques that were initially developed for the automobile industry, as the society itself shifted "to a consumer goods oriented economy."[3]

The car both transformed and often reinforced basic social institutions and traditional values. As Alexander Wilson pointed out, in the second half of the century:

> Planners and builders have organized most land development around the automobile. This had had enormous effects on how most of us see the landscape. It has also changed the look and feel of the land itself. The car has encouraged – indeed, insisted on – large-scale development: houses on quarter-acre lots, giant boulevards and expressways that don't welcome bicycles or pedestrians, huge stores or plazas surrounded by massive parking lots.[4]

From the way North Americans travel and the concept of the family vacation; to the way we worship – including Reverend Robert Schuller's pulpit surrounded by twenty-two acres of worshippers receiving "the Word" on their car radios; to the way we shop and the distant megacorporation malls that serve us; to the way we build, and the now-standard two-car garage, where one-third of a house's square footage is reserved to store cars, vans, or SUVs (and usually more than one at a time): all of this and more can be traced to the influence of our booming car culture. The now-standard strips of franchise operations of all sorts that form a kind of ugly oblong gateway to our cities are another manifestation. So too is the ubiquitous McDonald's – with its heady company goal of having "a restaurant within four minutes of everyone in the United States."[5]

The car's role in suburbanization is one of the most obvious of these transformations. By 1950 the automobile had not only pushed rural residents towards the city, but had also relocated 25 per cent of the

American people to the auto-dependent suburbs.[6] Probably fewer people are aware of the way in which "the automobile has literally turned the American house around," Vieyra suggests. "As the front yard became a small, very public auto dominated space, the family retreated to the rear yard (often fenced in) or 'garden,' with its patio which, replacing the front porch, was usually an extension of the family room, a new informal combination parlor and dining room."[7]

This and the other car-induced changes were bound to alter how Americans and Canadians would see themselves and transform their interactions, their sense of community as well as of personal freedom. Individual mobility became a hallmark of North American life. In the social history *Canadians in the Making*, written in the late 1950s, Arthur Lower turned his attention to a phenomenon he referred to as "the great god CAR":

> CAR threatened to turn us all into nomads, and his wheels, like Juggernaut, levelled every physical and psychical obstacle they met. They invaded every urban open space and threatened to destroy every blade of urban grass. They knocked down houses. They called imperiously for straight, wide roads to be carved out of our diminishing fertile fields. They tore up our precious peach orchards and ordained that factories for making new parts of CAR should be erected in their place.[8]

Holidaying was transformed. As Vieyra points out, "Auto-camping grew in popularity, appealing to an increasingly broad segment of society," and for Americans in general "it held the promise of breaking social barriers, rekindling an egalitarian spirit of democracy."[9] The informality of auto-camping, with the stories of expensive limousines and dilapidated touring cars parked alongside one another, while their bank president and labourer or farm owners socialized, would later give way to corporate chain-branding and AAA and CAA star rankings. Cabin and motel design became a marketing issue and not just a question of architecture. Roadside lodging followed changes in car design. The open-air tent houses/camps and the touring cars of the early years of automobility gave way to glass-enclosed cabins or motels and sedans. Daniel J. Boorstin beautifully captures this important change of seeing the world differently through the automobile's "moving 'picture window.'" Boorstin argues that the automobile's dominance and its accompanying cultural artifacts of superhighways, motels, drive-ins, and service centres make the description "landscape" no longer appropriate. He speaks instead of the "motorscape."[10]

When travellers first went out on the road, for overnight accommodation they tended to hitch a lean-to tent to the side of the car. Later, when auto-camping was replaced by the permanence and convenience of cabins, guests parked their cars, often in carport accommodations under the shelter of roofs, alongside the cabin being rented. Later tourist courts (often referred to as auto courts) would add large semi-circular and horseshoe-shaped driveways, open to and visible from the road, to this pattern of alternating individual cabins and parking slots. With the advent of motel architecture, the car was moved to an even more central position directly in front of the unit the driver occupied. Still later, beginning in the mid-1950s, a creative and variegated motel architecture would give way to a uniform standardization and the branding of corporate chain motels. All of this change and development was driven by the North American public's fascination with and adoption of the car.

As increasing automobility combined with highway construction and the building of the Interstate system, the travelling public's tastes in accommodations changed accordingly. Between 1937 and 1939 in the United States the number of travellers staying at motor courts more than doubled, rising from 12.5 per cent to 26 per cent, while during the same period the number of travellers taking rooms at traditional hotels dropped from 61 per cent to 46 per cent.[11] By 1950 motels had an estimated income of $450 million and were accommodating 59 per cent of U.S. travellers – while hotels were taking in only 36 per cent of the market. The car and the corporate structures that it spawned, fanning out from Detroit, were at the centre of change. As each prevailing design gave way to the next, from tent camps to motels, the automobile was taken into account. The car had secured its special place.

By the time the motel was in full swing, in the mid-1950s, car ownership had become less of a privileged luxury item and more of an expected necessity. Even in Canada, where automobile mesmerization lagged at least slightly behind the insatiable appetite of the car-buying U.S. public, a steep increase in car ownership marked the postwar period. Between 1945 and 1952 vehicle registrations more than doubled, and by 1964 they had doubled again. In 1957 one-third of middle-income families ($2,000 to $3,000 annual incomes) owned a vehicle (often a used car), with nearly one-tenth of the families of a higher socio-economic station owning two cars. The one in seven Canadians who owned a car in 1941 had become one in five by 1951 and then one for every 3.3 persons by 1961 and 2.4 by 1971.[12] Automobile ownership raced far ahead of population growth. In brief, the car boom matched the baby boom and then some.

Automobility, Democracy, and the Promise of Freedom

According to Cotton Seiler, in his investigation of anxiety and automobility during the Cold War 1950s period in the United States, "The key theme in the literature of automobility was self-determination."[13] This theme can be found in the words of early American writers such as Ralph Waldo Emerson and Walt Whitman and was restated for a larger audience by Jack Kerouac in his modern classic *On the Road* (1957). For Seiler, the automobile played a key role in supporting the importance of "mobility" in an American value system grounded on a connection between freedom and democracy. He discusses various views/definitions of autonomy, emphasizing the point that many observers of the North American scene view individual freedom and mobility as equatable, equal sides of an equation representing democracy.[14]

But not every potential consumer was to experience the freedom of the freeway and automobility. Even among those with the money to participate, some were more free than others, and not everyone was invited to party in the malls at the end of the off-ramps. Entire groups, such as women and African-Americans, were left to experience a pedestrian freedom closely aligned with their second-class citizenship and class position.[15]

The excluded groups lived what Herbert Marcuse termed "repressive tolerance," their potential freedom turned into "unfreedom," the opposites that Marcuse analyzed and warned us about.[16] These groups experienced a discipline, thoroughly analyzed by Michel Foucault, that was disguised as individualism.[17]

Hal Niedzviecki has shown how corporatized mass entertainment disciplines individuality by turning it into its opposite, conformity under the disguise of "I'm special" taken to an extreme.[18] The irony and the paradox in Niedzviecki's conformity are that the more people attempt to assert their special individuality, the less special they become. To put it another way, the more the conformity to specialness, the less likely that a person will experience individualistic privileges such as withdrawal, the postmodern replacement of the capital "I" with the small "i" of one truly able to author unique experiences. Instead, the emphasis of "I'm special," like other types of conformity, often leads to identification as a member of marginalized groups marked by gender, class, ethnicity, and colour.

This conundrum is beautifully illustrated in the 2005 movie *Crash*, where the combination of being black, sexually playful, and driving a late-model expensive car brings an African-American SUV driver, a successful television/movie director, and his wife to the racist attention of a white police officer. The entertainment-industry man and his wife become the evening's entertainment for the officer, who demonstrates to the couple that no matter how successful they have become they are not free – as in independent from their marginalized group or the authority of the larger social system. As Seiler points out:

> From the beginning of the automobile age, the ostensibly universal prerogative of free access and passage was generally denied to African-American motorists – if not by the public road itself, then by the private services and facilities, both public and private, which sustained travelers.... For African-Americans automobility entailed both liberation and threat: the automobile promised escape and power, but it also made its occupants possible targets of terror.[19]

Discipline was the daily lived experience of many African-Americans who were willing to risk the racist dangers that went with separate-but-not-equal travelling[20] in exchange for the upward mobility into the middle class that the practice of automobility seemed to promise. In the 1950s American males were being challenged by corporate advertising to fight the increasing feminization, the domestication, of American culture and character (signified, for instance, in the other-direction of the Lonely Crowd). The media touted automobility and the do-it-yourself movement as examples of how the new man might recapture both his individuality and manhood by conquering new frontiers. However, there was a differentiated audience response grounded in the colour of one's skin. That is, for African-American males the car as a resurrection or restatement of manhood was less about the cross-country journey Kerouac-style, say, from Connecticut to California, and more about travelling from the lower (working) classes into the middle class.

Paul Gilroy focuses upon "auto-autonomy as a means of escape, transcendence and perhaps even resistance" among U.S. blacks: "It raises the provocative possibility that their distinctive history of propertylessness and material deprivation has inclined them towards a disproportionate investment in particular forms of property that are publicly visible and the status that corresponds to them."[21] And perhaps car ownership does command an important measure of respect and recognition. But whether African-Americans in recent years have been able as a group to buy their way out of their subordinate position, thereby reversing the effects of American racism, is open to question. Certainly *Crash*-like scenes are replayed hundreds of times daily across the country.

At the end of the twentieth century African-Americans were spending some $45 billion on cars "and related products and services" and making up 30 per cent of the automotive-buying public, while forming only 12 per cent of the U.S. population.[22] Still, even that level of participation in the automotive culture and industry cannot erase the historical record. Gilroy presents some of this record: the reality of segregated dealing in automobiles, the racist white supremacy of Henry Ford – his anti-Semitic connection to Hitler and their mutual admiration for one another – and the racist use of boxing champion Jack Johnson's loss to Barney Oldfield in a celebrated 1910 black against white car race to question and reaffirm so-called "inferior" mental abilities of the champion and blacks in general.

At the beginning of the twentieth century, according to Gilroy, it looked as if:

> For African-American populations seeking ways out of the lingering shadows of slavery, owning and using automobiles supplied one significant

The Party Hits the Road: A Ticket to Ride • 47

means to measure the distance travelled toward political freedoms and public respect. Employed in this spirit, cars seem to have conferred or rather suggested dimensions of citizenship and status that were blocked by formal politics and violently inhibited by informal codes.[23]

Later, as Gilroy notes, "The same freedom-seeking people would be confined to the disabling options represented by rural poverty on one side and inner city immiseration on the other." "White flight" away from urban centres was both "accomplished" and "premised" on the automobile. Even when black agency in the form of customizing attempted to remake cars as symbols of freedom and resistance, the experimentation was less a personalized statement and much more, as is the case with "black" music and other artistic expressions, a statement turned into "race-coded particularity."[24]

For Gilroy, "The cars and their antisocial sociality redrew the lines between public and private, impacted profoundly upon gender relations, illuminated class divisions, interrogated selfishness, and tested the mutuality of sub-urban residential locations that were increasingly remote from places where work could be found."[25] In the final analysis, "driving while black" is testimony to the shortcomings of America's democratic experiment, the unfreedom experienced by those particular groups excluded from Seiler's "republic of drivers."

Women, of all colours and ethnic backgrounds, constitute another excluded group. Their experience of automobility is testimony to how every aspect of our culture is gendered. Seiler points out that "the republic of drivers" is an abstract(ed) community – and this abstraction not only features and foregrounds but also hides class, race/ethnic, and gender discrimination. He argues that the practice of automobility fits well with "the heroic narration of American history [not herstory] as the story of a mobile, individualistic, and dynamic nation" of vision.[26] It is automobility, perhaps more than any other phenomenon, that defines and sets apart the American way of life from life elsewhere. Automobile use and ownership, then, can be roughly thought of as a more universal equivalent to James Twitchell's "emotional credential" (a credential of both equality and adult status to be taken seriously), a credential that does not depend on formal schooling, on university attendance or graduation.[27]

The promise of automobility as an agent of democracy, individual freedom, and renewal melds with a sort of permanent American mindset grounded in the experience of pioneers and the narrative of expansion that they helped to create. The automobility story, like that of the pioneers, is a story of masculine prerogative that has, as numerous feminist scholars have noted, systematically and systemically sidelined women on the freeway shoulders and in the passenger seats.[28]

An American woman was first issued a licence to drive in 1899, and ten years later Alice Huyler Ramsey drove three other women coast-to-coast across the United States. These were the exceptions, though, in a car use and ownership culture that would characterize much of the twentieth century. Within the scope of this culture – leaving aside the degree of freedom to be had in an automobility where the freeway itself structures driving experiences – women were to be found at freedom's margins, well hidden by men and their money, and their passions. Women's automobility in this abstract republic of drivers, like other aspects of their identity, was to be found and subsumed under the identities of particular men – husbands, fathers, brothers, lovers. Women as a group were to be submissive to men, who in general – with missionary-position zeal – defended masculine privilege for all it was worth. Part of this involved viewing women drivers as something of a threat. This threat idea permeates our culture and will not easily die. Indeed, there is a well entrenched fear that our society has become devalued as it becomes increasingly feminized. Arguments about the "would-be men" desires of women who wanted to drive supplemented what for decades remained as a set of clichéd and disparaging jokes and stories about the incompetence of women at the wheel. More subtle help in men's fight to protect their turf came from mass media advertising, and all of this was grounded upon the standard sexist "naturalist" stereotypes regarding feminine frivolity, domesticity, passivity, irrationality, weakness, and inferiority rooted in biology. For many long decades, then – and certainly for the first half of the twentieth century and more – women were second-class citizens in the driving republic.

Change in this regard came only gradually, partly with the help of statistical evidence from insurance company records indicating women's driving competence and partly from the money that women began to earn from increased large-scale participation in paid labour

The Party Hits the Road: A Ticket to Ride • 49

outside the home. Something of a new automobility self came into being. Women moved from the passenger to the driver's seat. Soccer moms, their chauffeur status reproducing the stereotypical position of African-American males minus the paycheque, became central figures in advertising attempts to push van sales to new highs. Yet even a cursory observation of cars and drivers on family outings and during rush-hour traffic shows a continuing preponderance of men at the wheel – a practice supported by images of automobility in magazines, film, television, and other popular culture representations. These observations and images reveal just how much further women as a group will need to travel to attain a rough equality of economic and social opportunity and condition with white men and a significant portion of black males.

The parallels between automobility and football are instructive. Football even more so than automobility keeps women on the periphery. Women, in the equivalent of "riding shotgun," often serve as advertising models draped over and pitching the latest Detroit offering. Their football presence ranges from sidekick fans to sideline reporters and cheerleading dancers. The cheerleaders are allowed to be close to the action but are permitted to step inside the white lines only during specified breaks when the male players are not present, usually during pre-game and half-time spectacles as decorative add-ons – in something of the fashion of automobile hood ornaments.

Hot-Rodders and Consumer Conformity: Play Becomes Work

Hot-rodders have been a third and much smaller marginalized group in the story of automobility. Denney's University of Chicago student Gene Balsley, a hot-rodder himself, provided an early and close observation and analysis of the subculture, countering the prevailing 1950 image of hot-rodders as delinquent and disrespectful. Indeed, Balsley showed how their rebuilding of the standard Detroit issue offered a qualitative critique, a thoughtful and profitable addition, to both the automobile subculture and the larger socio-economic arrangements: "In general, the hot rodder protests against the automobile production and merchandising which fail to give the public a sufficiently wide range of models to permit judgments of value." For Balsley, the very scale of Detroit's parts industry – which in 1949 amounted to "a cool eight million per year gross income" – suggested "the huge scale of the hot rodder's protest."[29]

Balsley recognized that hot-rod culture was more than simply an engineering or design protest against Detroit: "The hot-rod culture has been called an attack on existing channels of expression – channels which grant success and acclaim only to those who fulfill certain occupational roles."[30] Denney himself cited the importance of hot-rod culture beyond its most obvious effects on production. He noted the hot-rodders' leadership in trying out new features, arguing that their usefulness to Detroit might lie "more in the field of consumption pioneering than in technological advance."[31]

Tom Wolfe, another keen observer of this marginal scene, recognized the influence of hot-rod culture, its power to reach beyond the boundaries of the subculture. His immensely popular 1966 book *The Kandy-Kolored Tangerine-Flake Streamline Baby* was a collection of his articles analyzing the culture-makers of the mid-twentieth century. It took its title (with its surrealistic style typical of the times) from his chapter telling the stories of the hot-rodders he had encountered in California. He writes of the hot-rodder's freedom, a customizing freedom different from the liberation promised by the open road designated as freeway. He profiles two customizers of the postwar period, George Barris and Ed Roth. Both of them, like most hot-rod customizers, were more artists than engineers. Barris used his high-school, college, and art school education to combine mechanical drawing, shop, and "free art." Wolfe describes his modifications of factory-produced models as "baroque" and "baroque modern" in design. He and his customizing buddies "were doing things Detroit didn't do until years later – tailfins, bubbletops, twin headlights, concealed headlights, 'Frenched' headlights, the low-slung body itself." The Detroit manufacturers apparently got the inspiration for some twenty designs from Barris alone. One example was exhaust pipes coming out through the rear bumper or fender. Another was "the bullet-shaped, or breast-shaped if you'd rather, front bumpers on the Cadillac."[32] This act of customizing in the manner of the Cadillac bumper transforms automobility from auto-identity to auto-erotic.

Barris wound up making money as a consultant to Detroit; and both Barris and Roth found, as did other famous artists – say, Picasso –

that the reproduction business was lucrative, with AMT Models and Revel reproducing their creations. Creativity, however, was at risk. Customizing became, to some extent, rationalized and routinized as many undercapitalized and often broke customizers were forced into being more open to market co-optation. Still, as Denney noted, the subcultural context of hot-rodding remained strong enough to continue offering members a unique world of experience. In the customizing body shops, "where customers and operators speak with a critical vocabulary all their own," the artists take the Detroit cars under their care and remove the ornaments and chrome.

> The man with money who is willing to spend it to make his new car a different car drives away with a "custom" model. And the young man with an old car and little money likewise gets a "personal" model with lines unlike those of other cars on the road. At this point, of course, when buyer criticism of standardization is more passive, the car-building impulse . . . becomes something else – an exercise in what David Riesman identifies as marginal differentiation.[33]

In the years since Denney wrote about "the plastic machines" and their customizers, the interest and membership in hot-rod culture have only increased. *Hot Rod* magazine, first published in 1948, continues to draw a wide readership. According to statistics provided by its parent company, the magazine conglomerate ABC, *Hot Rod*'s subscription earnings began to dip in the late 1990s, but its revenues on single-copy sales continued to hold steady at more than $4 million a year. While a preference for web-based technology and the information it provides surely plays a role in the magazine's drop in overall revenues, this same technology has undoubtedly been crucial in maintaining a vibrant hot-rod culture. The Internet and many websites, photo galleries, chat rooms, and blogs play a significant and sustaining role.

For example, StreetRodding.com features "30,000+ hot rods, street rods and classic car photos and classifieds" to whet the appetites of prospective buyers, while CruisinRods.com encourages do-it-yourselfers in how to "Build a Killer Hot Rod Start to Finish," advertising a "breakthrough new step by step book [that] shows you how!" Even more, if someone is really keen to hone his or her customizing skills (and, largely as a result of Internet accessibility, girls and women have become an increasing presence in hot-rod culture), you can tune into television's "Hot Rod University." Perhaps the history of this hot-rod subculture is your field of study, your thing. If so, you can leave the jalopyjournal.com website and your reading of *garage* magazine, a "rods & kustom kulture mag," behind to focus upon madfabricators.com, a website that bills itself as "old school hot rod culture." Or you might want to read *Hot Rod*'s version of the history and death of moonshine culture in an article on "Moonshine Runners & Cars They Drove." Perhaps a Hotrod-A-Rama rock music party or a hot-rod culture cruise and memorial festival is your thing. There is something for everyone. It's all there at your fingertips, on the Net.

Cottage industries and much website attention have grown up around the now infamous customizers profiled more than forty years ago by Wolfe: Ed "Big Daddy" Roth, and George Barris, "King of the Kustomizers." Roth was especially influential with his comic-book-type character Rat Fink, a repulsive and menacing rodent who served as anti-hero to Disney's Mickey Mouse and whose family included Drag Nut, Mother's Worry, and Mr. Gasser. All of these characters, like his early customized cars, "The Outlaw," "The Beatnik Bandit," and "Rotar," gave Roth an iconic-like status among alienated teenagers who knew they didn't fit in but wanted to feel good about who they were. His cartoon creations (later picked up by surf musicians, punk, garage, and "alternative" bands for covers and T-shirts) and their audiences recall both Denney's use of comic strips and cartoons ("Smilin' Jack" and "Gasoline Alley") as a means of understanding youth and cultural trends, as well as his characterization of hot-rodders as "a salon of the refused."

Customizer Roth, whom Wolfe described as "a rather thoroughgoing bohemian" who "kept turning up at the car shows in a T-shirt," was a colourful and cynical, charismatic leader who resisted co-optation. Characterized by Wolfe as "the Salvador Dali of the customizing movement – a surrealist in his designs, a showman by temperament, a prankster" – Roth held out against the too-squeaky-clean image of hot-rod culture being promoted by the establishment National Hot Rod Association. He was keeping "alive the spirit of alienation and rebellion that is so important to the teen-age ethos that customizing grew up in."[34] For Roth, a customizer of cars and silkscreen T-shirts, familiar with tattoos and body art, difference made a difference. It was important to be different, and Roth certainly was.

An emphasis on the importance of difference is another way of talking about prestige and status. Wolfe's observations – like those of Denney and Balsley – are grounded in the realization that the automobile is something more than simply McLuhan's extension of our feet. These writers (McLuhan included) recognize the auto as a signifier of prestige and a symbol of status; the car as a consumer item goes beyond Denney's wonderful reference to it as "a kind of daily apparel." Furthermore, as is the case with apparel and the fashion fad of the moment, the specific car that marks the first consumers of a particular model as being different becomes, under the guidance of corporate advertisers and the mass media, the new conformity. The same holds true when that car is customized. Denney puts it this way:

> Just as young people use sports as a way of grasping at the latent meaning of folkway in the United States, they use the cast-off cars of a rich economy to play a quasi-adult game with them. The game is at first a revolt against the market place and the rhetoric of advertising; later it becomes a group process richly invested with public values, even at the expense of the individualism with which it began.[35]

"I am special" – in part because of my purchase and reworking of consumer goods – becomes not so special after all. In 1957 Denney summarized this confusion as it surfaced for hot-rodders: "It is far more difficult now than in 1946 for a hot-rodder to know whether he is in the game for fun or for business."[36] The statement recalls Denney's distinction between the unpaid amateur, whose investment in task is stimulated by creative curiosity as a labour of love, and the salaried professional, whose training turns this love into soul-destroying "assigned curiosity"[37] suitable to bureaucratic employment. The confusion between being in the game for business or for fun (play) also connects to and is a reminder of the classic work by German sociologist Max Weber (1864–1920), whose writings focused on the bureaucratic rationalization of authority and capitalism. Innovative difference and any special status that it might create among hot-rodders and others regularly become, like Weber's charismatic leaders, routinized and standardized. Both play and work become commodified; the boundaries that formerly separated them become confused in their continual redefinition.

CHAPTER 4

Big Games

"The Decline of Lyric Sport"

> The imagery of competition, as represented in the Big Game and in media interpretation of the Big Game, contributes to the system of expectations holding among various parts of society. Sport can be studied as social imagery – spectacle from which the media draw symbols that are then employed in the supreme court of folkway.
>
> – Denney, *The Astonished Muse*, p.98

EACH YEAR, AROUND THE END OF THE FIRST WEEK OF JANUARY, the Bowl season proper comes to its inevitable completion. What used to be a few days of games has now turned into nearly three weeks (with another three-plus weeks added on if you count all the January all-star games) and a grand total of twenty-eight bowl games. The corporate sponsors of these games span a wide range: everything from sports equipment companies to car (new, rental, and maintenance), high-tech, electronics, computer, phone, communication, and delivery companies; from the finance industry of banks, credit unions, credit card, and insurance companies to chain hotels and restaurants; even manufacturers of potato chips and hair-care products. A conservative estimate of the bowl take in 2005–06 – a season that ended with the new Rose Bowl winner and national champion Texas defeating the previous year's champ University of Southern California (USC) – was a total pay-out in the neighbourhood of $100 million.[1] It's the kind of money that must warm the hearts of the corporate friends of president and Texas fan George W. Bush – from the Lone Star State to Hollywood and

• 57

beyond. And it's a far cry from Denney's estimate of a 1950 *complete-season gate* for all of the U.S. college football industry of $103 million, a sum that today is in itself routinely approached and often exceeded by Texas, USC, Oregon, and nearly every big-time college program on every single Saturday during the season.²

That today's corporations play a gigantic role in a U.S. college football industry that is big business is no longer news. But there was a time not too long ago when there were no corporate sponsors and games were poorly attended. In less than seventy-five years American college football went from being a leisure-time extracurricular activity observed by a handful of local spectators to a great, popular spectacle with a national and global audience. It became part of big-money high-profit investment in programs and highly trained players whose student-athlete status often emphasizes the athletic over the studious. (See, for instance, their choice of academic majors and courses, grade-point averages, and especially graduation rates.) This unique American game has come a long way from the industrial folkways that marked its beginnings.

Beginnings: Football Rules and Industrial America

When Princeton and Rutgers met each other on the field in 1869 in the first intercollegiate football match, their game more closely resembled English football (or soccer) than what we would today recognize as American (or Canadian) football. Succeeding matches in the 1870s involving other Eastern schools were also played under soccer rules. In May 1874, when McGill University travelled from Montreal to play two games with Harvard, the teams used Harvard's adapted London soccer rules for one contest, while the other was played under the Rugby Union code followed by the Canadians. Two years later, in 1876, when Princeton and Pennsylvania (soccer rules) got together with Harvard and Yale (rugby rules) to create the Intercollegiate Football Association, they adopted a common rule book to govern play. This historic meeting set the stage for rule modifications over the next thirty-five years, introducing a new configuration that would fashion, from its soccer and rugby beginnings, a distinctive brand of American football. As Michael Oriard points out, the uniqueness of this version, which separated it from both rugby and soccer, derived "from two crucial factors: the organization of time and the rule for possession of the ball."[3]

An 1880 rule creating the scrimmage line, and thus a definitive beginning and end to the action for each play, was joined by another rule established in 1882, the five-yards-in-three-plays rule, which granted possession of the ball to a specific side dependent upon the offensive team's progress toward the goal. These two rules formed the centrepiece, the basis, for various other rules and changes, such as permitting blockers to precede or to lead ball carriers and defenders to tackle below the waist.

Early in the 1913 season forward-passing, legal since 1906 but not yet utilized, would join running and kicking in a way that made use of the oval-shaped ball to transform the American game. Two Notre Dame players, Knute Rockne and Gus Dorais, unveiled the spiralling forward pass they had been working on during summer vacation to post an upset victory over the favoured West Point team. With the addition of this overhand downfield pass the modern American game, today's football as we know it, was essentially complete. Later, Rockne's success as a coach would be added to his playing resume. Rockne's notoriety for both creativity and discipline led Denney to refer to the sports stalwart as football's Henry Ford, thus placing him alongside another famous innovator and organizer of the period.

Today there is only minor tinkering with the rules, and yet the importance of rules and their studied revision remains. Rules were and are revised to make illegal certain new tactics that coaches and players use to subvert the intention and application of previous rules. But most importantly the many rules – sixty-five pages and fourteen thousand words covered the 1911 season[4] – and the numerous officials (referee, umpires, and judges) reflect more than the governance of the game: they reveal much about the cultural character of modern society. On the one hand all of this formal organization manages to satisfy a popular taste for the excitement of action-driven entertainment; on the other hand, the formalization also reveals a desire for standardization and centralization. The game's rule-bound, legalistic approach to play is conducive to the big business of entertainment that football has become.

Denney's description of business football as part of the industrialized order – of the way in which the game and its development fit neatly within prevailing "industrial folkways" – melds nicely with a view of the game espoused more than fifty years earlier by Walter Camp. Known as "the father of football at Yale," "the coach of coaches," and "the King of American football," Camp was widely acknowledged in newspapers and magazines of the day as the game's most recognized authority. As both an undergraduate and graduate student, while making his mark as Yale's leading running back from 1876 to 1882, Camp was involved in the codification of rules. He served for a total of twenty-eight years on the intercollegiate rules committee, and for nearly thirty years as graduate advisor to Yale's captains, and he personally selected the annual All-American teams for *Collier's Weekly* from 1889 until his death in 1925. Camp's voluminous football writings covered more than three decades and appeared in major periodicals and newspapers as well as in book form. All of this activity accompanied a forty-year business career spent with the New Haven Clock Company, where he eventually became president and chairman of the board.[5]

In football Camp envisaged the hierarchical structure of the industrial corporation. When overall strategy and individual plays were executed properly, the football team efficiently emulated the bureaucratic and rationally specialized corporate workforce. Camp's writings emphasized the importance of teamwork as a rationalized, integrated division of labour. For Camp, according to Oriard, "Football was a mirror of the corporation, a preparation for corporate success, and itself a corporate activity. Football was work, not play."[6] Camp once wrote that football's "great lesson" was that *"it teaches that brains will always win over muscle!"*[7]

The problem with mirrors is not only that the structure of the image is reversed, but also that the images are often distorted. Thus Camp found himself defending the infant American game against critics who saw it moving from gentlemanly conduct to vicious brutality, from amateurism to professionalism, from a university extracurricular activity and a timeout from scholarly endeavours to a centre-stage spectacle symbolic of higher education. They also saw it moving from a non-pecuniary leisure activity to a business marked by financial excess. As for brains, the game made it clear that they do not always triumph over brawn. Even Camp had to acknowledge that teamwork was often supplemented and sometimes supplanted by the superior skill and athleticism of the gridiron hero. Still, football in Camp's day relied heavily on rational organization, a teamwork informed by science. Football today, with its specialized skill development, two-platooning, special teams, and a small army of coaches aided by the latest in computerized technology, remains even more in the Camp mould as a "managed science," rather than an art.[8]

Football's development as an industry has been powered by the intelligence of two groups of off-field specialists: scientifically trained technologists and sports writers. The technologists saved football from its early critics who wanted to put an end to the game and its violence, but in doing so they promoted an equipment technology that helped to create an even more violent and thus a more popular game. During this same period sports writers reporting on both the on-field action and the social contexts within which that action occurred eventually created a mass audience, transporting football from its original location in regional games to the larger sites of a national spectacle.

Technologists and Scientific Football

By the turn of the nineteenth century American football had become increasingly violent, in large part due to the absence of an adequate offside rule. Permitting linemen and blockers to be in motion before the ball was snapped provided offences with a tactical and organizational advantage over stationary "sitting duck" defensive opponents. One result was the infamous, bruising and finally outlawed "flying wedge."[9] Technology played a major role in making the public aware of football violence, moving concern beyond the specifics of the wedge play.

Advances in the relatively new technology of photography led to pictorial sports coverage, photographic reporting, appearing on a daily basis in the newspapers. A particularly striking, graphic photograph of the bloodied face of Swarthmore's star lineman Bob Maxwell after a 1905 game against Pennsylvania caught the attention of President Theodore Roosevelt. A Harvard graduate, Roosevelt had in several publications promoted the virtues of "manly sport" as part of the character development required of gentlemen leaders from his aristocratic background. He was appalled by the Maxwell picture. Football brutality had been an issue all through the 1890s, and Roosevelt vowed to use his executive power to abolish football if immediate rule changes were not made to eliminate rough play.

Rule changes followed, and Roosevelt and Congress were kept at bay; however, as most observers realized, changes in rules could not rule out all football violence. Furthermore, and most importantly, as Denney pointed out a half-century later, an American ambivalence regarding physical violence ensured that zero tolerance could never be the goal:

> Americans fear and enjoy their aggression at the same time and thus have difficulty pinning down the inner meanings of external violence. The game of Rugby as now played in England is probably as physically injurious as American football was at the turn of the century. By contrast, American attitudes toward football demonstrate a forceful need to define, delimit, and conventionalize the symbolism of violence in sports.[10]

The technologists and their scientific advances fulfilled this need to set limits, to govern and control the emotional symbolism as well as the injurious reality of on-field violence.

One day not long ago I hefted the football shoulder pads worn by a friend's son and was struck by how light they were when compared with my memory of the heavy cardboard and cloth equipment that my friends and I had lugged onto the field when we played in the 1950s. Of course, the reduction in weight along with the increased impact protection of the latest innovations in plastic that mark today's football gear is not the only advancement in the technology of the sport. The university and professional playing fields themselves are today most often constructed of some artificial variant of Astroturf. This supposedly improved surface has consistently proven hazardous to players' legs – witness the proliferation of knee braces on players up front; on many teams they look less like an offensive line and more like the waiting lines outside an orthopedist's office. One thing the new field surfaces do is make player identification easier for fans, statisticians, and announcers, because the players' numbers are no longer obscured by

62 • *Fun & Games & Higher Education*

the dirt and mud that results from the natural grass field on a less-than-pleasant-weather day. They also ensure that the games can be played in or after bad weather, thus answering to the demands of the market.

In many of today's stadiums the weather and the resulting sloppy and injury-producing field conditions are no longer even factors, because the game is played indoors under a dome or roof offering protection from wind, sun, sleet, and snow. To match the modern stadium architecture, a phalanx of specialized coaches trained in the science of football now provides players with sophisticated game films and advance scouting reports on opponent weaknesses, strengths, and tendencies. Game-day action (sideline coaching was not officially legalized until 1967) is governed by high-tech communication devices and headsets delivering messages and digitalized stop-action sequential images of each play to sideline coaches and players from other coaches in booths high above the stadium turf. The often exhausted players glean what they can from the game intelligence and photos while reviving themselves with scientifically tested, healthy sport drinks, an extension of the training table started by Camp at Yale. Gulps of oxygen are also provided by sideline tanks, and in many outdoor stadiums sideline air conditioners or heating units are also used to counter prevailing weather conditions.

There is little doubt that the technology developed alongside the rule-governed science of football has had several beneficial effects. The high-tech conditions have protected players from both unnecessary wear and tear, and serious injury. Improvements over the years in the design and protection offered by the football helmet, to take but one example, have been well documented, as has the accompanying reduction in life-threatening and debilitating head, neck, and spinal cord injuries. Still, what often goes unrecognized is that these same improvements permit body impacts of greater intensity to be given as well as taken. Later rule changes prohibited the violent and dangerous practice of spearing – that is, leading with the helmeted head first when tackling – as well as tackling by grabbing the face mask. But while the advances in technology and rule changes have helped to manage the violence of the modern game, they have also maintained the violence, and in effect increased it.

Sportscasters often play up this violence, proving more than willing to give fans yet another jolt. For instance, I clicked onto a major Canadian sports network recently and happened to catch the anchor on a daily news update just prior to a commercial break. In a moment of obviously eager anticipation – there was a lift in his voice – he was asking his audience to stay tuned for what was to come, the "best" recent hits in football: "Tighten your chin strap. We've got a head jarring edition of the 'hit parade' coming up."

It turned out that the "hit parade" is a regular feature, and it is but one small example of many instances in which football violence is celebrated and encouraged. The acceptance and commodification of violence are not surprising. They can be viewed as a logical and expected extension of a wedding between science and technology that encourages us to militarize and objectify players and each other. I am not talking about the most obvious connections, such as the manner in which the game and its language ("field general" quarterbacks, defences that "blitz"[kreig] the opposition, "two-platoon" systems, linemen in the "trenches") suggest a warlike military demeanour. Rather, I am referring here to the manner in which we as a culture view the players, and to the way in which most players eventually come to think about themselves.

Don DeLillo explores that kind of mindset in his engaging football novel *End Zone*.[11] Early in the book the narrator, Gary, fakes a leg injury and limps to the sideline for a break, where he engages in an exchange with the team's kicker, Jackmin:

"Work," he [Jackmin] shouted past me.
   "Work, you substandard industrial robots. Work, work, work, work."
   "Look at them hit," I said. "What a pretty sight when Coach says hit, we hit. It's so simple."
   "It's not simple, Gary. Reality is constantly being interrupted. We're hardly even aware of it when we're out there. We perform like things with metal claws. But there's the other element. For lack of a better term I call it the psychomythical. That's a phrase I coined myself."
   "I don't like it. What does it refer to?"
   "Ancient warriorship," he said. "Cults devoted to pagan forms of technology. . . . "

"Wuuurrrrk. Wuuuurrrrk."

"Hobbs'll throw to Jessup now," I said. "He always goes to his tight end on third and short inside the twenty. He's like a retarded computer."

Later on another teammate, Joost, in a sideline conversation with Gary, elaborates upon football's technological future, offering a high-tech version that does justice to today's computerized game:

"This whole game could be played via satellite. They could shoot signals right down here. We'd be equipped with electronic listening devices. Transistor things sealed into our headgear. We'd receive data from the satellites and run our plays accordingly. The quarterback gets one set of data. The linemen get blocking patterns. The receivers get pass routes. Ek cetera. Same for the defense. Ek cetera."

"Who sends the data?" I said.

"The satellites."

"Who feeds the satellites?"

"A computer provides the necessary input. There'd be a computerized data bank of offensive plays, of defensive formations, of frequencies. What works best against a six-one on second down and four inside your thirty? The computer tells the satellite. The satellite broadcasts to the helmet. There'd be an offensive satellite and a defensive satellite."

Players reduced to computerized robots: this is a high-tech, cleaned-up version of the physical-psychological training that former player Gary Shaw made public in his telling exposé of Texas college football. Shaw wrote about how training and treatment reduced players to "Meat on the Hoof" and encouraged all those connected with the game to think that it was worth the gamble to grab any slight advantage, technical and otherwise, that might lead to greater success.[12]

Phil Knight, perhaps the most famous alumnus of the University of Oregon, and his world-renown and infamous (for its labour practices) Nike corporation provide another example of this same phenomenon. In 2003 Nike – which had previously introduced the tearaway jersey – came up with "cooling vests" and made these experimental vests available to the Oregon Duck football team for possible use in an away game against the Mississippi State Bulldogs. The game date was

August 30, a time when temperatures in Starkville, Mississippi, are regularly in a humid 80-to-90-Fahrenheit-degree range, and the vest, a bladder-like T-shirt worn under the shoulder pads, was designed to be connected to a sideline compressor so that cool dehumidified air could be blown on the players. When Mississippi State coach Jackie Sherrill got wind of this innovation, so to speak, he was understandably concerned. He let the press know that his school, also under contract with Nike, had not been offered this latest equipment, at least until he asked about it. In the end, after Nike delivered an eleventh-hour shipment to Mississippi State in an effort to equalize things, the vest controversy was just so much hot air. The ESPN2 television schedule pushed the game from afternoon to evening and neither the victorious Ducks nor the Bulldogs found it necessary to wear the cooling vests. Most interesting, however, were Sherrill's comments following his initial statement of concern, comments praising how great Nike's participation had been for college sports and offering assurances that the vest controversy would not disrupt Mississippi State's relationship with the company.

Nike's design and marketing of footwear, apparel, equipment, and accessory products produced annual 2004 revenues of more than $13 billion – the kind of money and clout, not to mention the free samples and supplies, that keeps Sherrill and other coaches as well as players loyal to Nike and founder Phil. Nike is a major player in the sports arena, but many other corporations are also interested in the profits to be made through association with big-time college football – witness the high stakes in the college bowl season.

Sportswriters, and Football as National Spectacle

It was the sports writers of the late nineteenth century who propelled football from a local campus activity to national spectacle. In their game coverage they were less interested in documenting what actually transpired on the field than in emphasizing the social life surrounding the game. The popular press of the time created stories of football within a cultural text of possible representations and interpretations that brought the audience in as part of the emerging spectacle of sport as entertainment.

Prior to the 1880s, football coverage in the New York press and elsewhere was minimal, a reproduction and extension of the sparse crowds attending games. But between 1880 and the end of the century, as Oriard documents, increases in the number of newspapers – and in their readership and football coverage – combined to push a parallel growth in the game's popularity. The very first Thanksgiving Day football game in New York was held, for instance, in 1880, when the city had a population of 1.9 million; attendance at the game was 5,000. At that time the city had thirty-three daily newspapers, with a combined circulation of 814,000, and twenty-six Sunday papers, with a total circulation of 580,000. Only nine years later, in 1889, the number of papers had grown to fifty-five, and their circulation had more than tripled, reaching 1.78 million; there were thirty-two Sunday papers, with a circulation of 1.1 million. The Thanksgiving Day game that year drew 25,000 spectators from a population of 2.4 million. As Oriard points out, "By 1889, three daily papers were sold for every four citizens." Oriard quotes historian Michael Schudson, who calculated that at the time "one New Yorker in every two bought a Sunday paper."[13]

Despite the large growth in attendance at that Thanksgiving Day game – which pitted Yale against Princeton at the Berkeley Oval – a large portion of the crowd, Oriard figured, would have come from Princeton and New Haven, which meant that probably no more than one New Yorker in two hundred went out to watch the actual game. "In other words," he concluded, "the overwhelming majority of football's emerging audience discovered football not from the grandstand but from the daily press."[14]

In the papers by the 1890s, game descriptions of a few paragraphs had given way to multiple columns and entire pages. Joseph Pulitzer's *World* and William Randolph Hearst's *Journal* featured special sports sections complete with banner headlines and many diagrams, woodcuts, line drawings, and illustrations. Not only did they preview the games, but within hours of the final whistle the papers produced several different Saturday evening editions. Newspaper owners and editors used the latest in printing technology to build drama by presenting game-day action in a sequential and timely manner to a waiting and eager audience. Hearst hired the best writers of the day (the likes of Richard Harding Davis and Stephen Crane) to cover the big games.

"Game Day" hype, then, did not begin with television's ESPN and other network purveyors of today's college football.

But what exactly was being covered by the nineteenth-century popular press? What were reporters writing that appealed to a broad cross-section of non-college-educated social groups, thereby simultaneously increasing both newspaper circulation and interest in football? To answer simply but accurately, they were writing mostly about the social atmosphere surrounding the game, with less about the game itself – a point that Oriard emphasizes in his description of the development of football's narrative formula:

> Bracketed between the *Herald*'s or *World*'s long and colorful accounts of pregame and postgame festivity, were actual reports of the games themselves. In fact, *embedded within this extravagant social context, the descriptions of the games had to be comparably enhanced to seem worthy of provoking so much expense and enthusiasm.*[15]

Play-by-play coverage could not emerge until after the introduction of discrete plays, a reality made possible by the possession rule of 1880 and the five-yard rule of 1882. Still, for years after these rule changes came into effect football reporting was less about on-field action and more about bonfires and other pre-game and post-game celebrating – complete with published lists of revellers arrested. The features included the changing moods of the crowd and who exactly was in attendance – their social-class backgrounds and their manner of arrival, and what these spectators were wearing. They might speak of the colourful uniforms of the players, or of the women in attendance, or the shopping opportunities as well as the colourful decorating of the retail shops in the days leading up to the game. By interpreting rather than chronicling the action, the sportswriters of the day created narratives of the game as a social event larger and more spectacular than the game itself.

It was this football-as-social narrative that propelled the game from a localized regional event to national spectacle. In the Pacific Northwest, for example, the *Oregonian*, the daily newspaper of Oregon's largest city, Portland, found itself with little local product to cover in the way of football, with only club teams and some fledgling college and university teams playing a brand of football that was not up to Eastern standards. *Oregonian* reporters thus turned to the East, to Thanksgiving Day and Ivy League games played 3,000 miles away, across the country. Their coverage not only provided evidence of a homogenized narrative formula, a sameness of description and technique emulating and reproducing the technical robot-like science undergirding the game's on-field development, but also taught readers, potential fans, how to read or interpret the game. In his study of one game – the 1887 Thanksgiving Day Harvard-Yale match – Oriard concludes: "There's only one thing missing here: the game. Football here is entirely a social event."[16]

As a social event to be interpreted, the story of football can be told in a variety of ways: as science and technical innovation with a good measure of bureaucratic organization thrown in; as a story of heroic manliness; or as a lesson in ethics, a morality play. All of these readings can encompass a subtext of warfare and battle scenarios as well as of nationalism and patriotism.

Perhaps college football is a story of amateurism and the leisure-time activities of the upper class – a university-educated elite at play; or of amateurism beset by the capitalistic market values of an encroaching professionalism. Perhaps the reading is one of female exclusion and subordination or of ethnic immigration and discrimination. As Denney puts it in *The Astonished Muse*, "There is an element of class identification running through American football since its earliest days, and the ethnic origin of players invites theorizing about the class dimensions of football." Denney sees the "changes in football strategy and ethos" as something that ran parallel to the changes in the rules of the game: "All these developments are to be seen as part of a configuration that includes changes in coaching, in the training of the players, and in the no less essential training of the mass audience."[17]

In this "essential training" the brains and writings of sports reporters have clearly shaped the game of football every bit as much as the brawn and skills of the players themselves. My own choice of story, following Denney, is to see football as a class narrative of upward social mobility. "Increasingly," Denney pointed out in 1957, "football's major rationale as a part of higher education is that it plays a part in the American class-mobility system."[18] From this point of view, what we have is a community narrative of solidarity and togetherness combined not just with the all-important pursuit of higher education but also with a corporate narrative of business success. Interestingly, these narratives come together in a particular form, the tailgate party, a celebration that joins college football with the automobile. It is football as social occasion. To use the title of a Denney article, the culture surrounding American college football represents "a feast of strangers" whose needs regarding sociability help to transform them into festival celebrants who often become friends. "Have the convivial gatherings of Americans changed in their nature?" Denney asked, as he pondered "the great overlapping waves of immigration that once filled American boarding houses with that rough sociability that could well be described as a feast for strangers, by strangers, and of strangers?"[19]

CHAPTER

Tailgating

"A Feast of Strangers"

> The sociability of stranger with stranger is both modeled and purveyed by the entertainers of the culture, those whose performances bring large audiences of strangers together and whose enactments suggest a stance that can be shared by those who witness their performance. In our time, the range and potency of these celebrities has been multiplied by the mass media in a way that is all too well known. Its stars include athletes and sportsmen as entertainers and as setters of a leisure style of interaction.
>
> – Denney, "Feast of Strangers," p.262

I am up shortly after 5:30 A.M. My hosts, a cousin of mine and his wife, tell me that an early start is imperative. By the time the late summer sun makes its appearance, we are out on I-5, the second-busiest Interstate highway in the United States, making our way south from Olympia, Washington, to Eugene, Oregon. The occasion is the University of Oregon Ducks' second pre-season game against a much weaker University of Montana football team. Kickoff time: 12:30 P.M. The game promises to be a tuneup walkover for Oregon (and in the end it is, with the final score University of Oregon 47–Montana 14), but for me the football itself is not the main attraction. I am returning to my birth state to observe the pageantry and the spectacle, and to party with the tailgaters.

When I came of age as a driver in the 1950s, to tailgate meant that when you were driving down the highway in your car you were following the car in front of you too closely. Some fifty years later to tailgate is also to party, and while the old definition may still nicely apply in the routine gridlock that occurs as a driver approaches the off-ramp to the stadium, today's tailgating is all about celebrating.

This morning's revelry, perhaps reveille given the hour, begins on I-5 with the cars themselves as they stream along the highway, and the parade-float manner in which they have been decorated. The Ducks' green and yellow school colours are everywhere. Drivers and passengers dressed in yellow jackets, green and yellow windbreakers, and baseball caps co-pilot standard sedans and plenty of outsized SUVs. Decorating their rides are UO flags in both colours, yellow duck feathers, pompoms, OREGON in bold letters on windows and bumpers, and back-window pillows and miniature mascots, plus several yellow Big-O trailer hitches and licence plates dressed in Oregon colours.

Of the cars going our way, a late-model Lexus is typical. It carries two middle-aged gentlemen and comes complete with school pennants flying on both sides of the car. There are two small plush-toy Ducks in the back window, and a large "Go Ducks" sign affixed to the passenger door. But as I survey the busy scene on the I-5 I can see that it is not just mid-life men who have set out on this expedition. As I examine these autos and the apparent road warriors within them, I am reminded that this is not just another convention of Legionnaires out for a good time. Whole families move forward in the passing lane.

Among the SUVs is a GMC Yukon matching the dark green of the Duck uniforms. The hefty vehicle flies two school-coloured flags on each side, complete with a roof rack bearing UO gear and two big "O"s, one stuck in the middle of the back window and one lower down overshadowing the Yukon logo. A Ford Expedition sports green flags on one side and yellow on the other, with yellow duck feathers sticking out from the doors and the trunk, a miniature UO football atop the radio antenna. The co-pilot passenger, dressed in a school windbreaker with his Duck baseball hat askew, is visibly relaxing on a bright yellow pillow as he snoozes.

A few SUVs and cars, though, are filled with "Beaver Believers" and are adorned with the black and orange colours of Oregon State University, the hated rival of the "Civil War" battles that mark the last Pacific-10 Conference game of each season for both teams. The OSU game has a later, 4:00 P.M., start, at Reser Stadium in Corvallis, about thirty-five miles from Eugene.

Our journey takes us past places of my youth. We have already stopped at one roadside rest area to take our bathroom break along with other football fans. For coffee we make another stop in my hometown birthplace of Portland, at a café favoured by my cousin and his wife. The pilgrimage continues as we overtake a Portland Brewers truck with big lettering on the side advertising its mission: "Beer To The Game." We pass by signs pointing to many Oregon towns familiar to me – Lake Oswego, Woodburn, Salem (the state capital, where I attended university as an undergraduate), Albany, Lebanon, Sweet Home, Harrisburg, Junction City, Florence, the mill town of North Springfield – and finally reach our journey's destination, the turnoff to Eugene and the "Holy Shrine" of Autzen Stadium, home of the Ducks.

Once the cars, the SUVs, and the RVs are released from gridlock and ease their way to the university area and its stadium, we manage to secure a parking spot within hailing distance of the gridiron. Then, on the one-mile walk from our parking spot to the stadium my attention turns from automobiles to the fans themselves and their parties; and a whole new array of Duck-decorated equipment and gadgets comes into play. Besides the standard party food, grills, and accompanying apparatuses, the various parking lots we traverse feature tents (more than one decorated with a big-screen TV), dining-room-size outdoor tables, chairs, awnings, temporary porches and fences, big balloons, seven-foot-high blow-up Duck mascots in the "front yard" – well, you get the idea. And all of this awash in the green and yellow school colours.

Apparently, several celebrations have already been in full swing for some time prior to this 10:30 A.M. hour. Couples toast and hoist a beer or a glass of champagne together while teenagers and guys in their twenties along with several fathers and their sons or daughters play catch with miniature Oregon footballs amidst the strong aromas of barbecues working their magic. Fragments of conversation drift across the crowded byways – queries about the beer and pop cooler, the state of the burgers on the grill, the desire for another beer-basted bratwurst, a declaration by one fan that she is now on to her second Bloody Mary, where to find a favourite hoodie, compliments on game-day outfits.

The outfits almost defy description. Again green and yellow is omnipresent – all manner of brightly coloured headgear (baseball caps, golf visors, rain hats, ventilated brim hats, ivy-league caps, hard hats, wizard hats, wigs), shirts (T-, golf, turtleneck, sport polo, rugby, Hawaiian), jackets and hoodies, windbreakers and rain slickers, the green and yellow striped socks/leggings favoured by coeds, school-coloured Mardi-Gras beads and island leis, glasses and headphones with Duck insignia. Many students have obviously spent a fair amount of time early that morning painting their faces in school colours. As I round a corner of the parking lot in our walk I nearly flatten a costumed male in his twenties, perhaps early thirties, with a Duck hard hat on. His headgear serves for me as a representation of the social-class relations of football itself, the attendant Big Game spectacle, and, of course, the tailgate parties themselves.

Some ninety minutes before kickoff we finally reach the walkway surrounding the stadium. Our first stop is the Moshofsky Center, a huge indoor practice facility – and more – adjacent to the stadium. The Center doubles as a venue for game-day activities and special functions, and I want to be a participant-observer of what has been described as "the largest indoor [tailgate] party in North America." There are less than ten thousand-plus fans inside on this day – the opponent is not important enough, and it is early September: classes have not yet begun. Still, the party is on, and I blame a combination of crowd contagion and the television-mandated early start for my ordering and consuming an initial micro-brew well before the proverbial noon-hour finish line of restraint.

Again a word picture can hardly do justice to the scene inside the Center. On one side of this large building are places to buy drinks (a variety of beer and wine) and food with a capital F: the usual array of burgers and sausages and, for the more adventurous, a cajun chicken caesar wrap. For those seeking football-approved food, there is Game Day Chili Cheese Nachos or Goal Line Garlic Fries. They are tasty. For those needing the stamp of coach or ex-player authority, Coach Bellotti's Bar-B-Que or Coach Schaffeld's American Grill will provide your burger, and The Wild Duck, owned by ex-UO quarterback Chris Miller, will serve you up a Fighting Duck Philly Cheese Steak.

Covering the walls are action and still pictures of former Oregon greats arranged under captions such as "The Tough," "Blitz This Offensive Line," "Mayhem" (featuring three fierce-looking linebackers), and "Speed." But it is on the other side of this vast arena, opposite the drinks and food, where most of the action is taking place. On stage is a live band playing some cool R&B and funk. Earlier, apparently, there was the player walk-through – we missed it. The main attraction now, when the band takes a break, is the ear-splitting entrance of the Duck mascot, looking very Donald and Disneyesque with his big orange duckbill and matching leggings, astride his revved-up motorcycle. This heralds the entrance of the Duck rally squad – the scantily clad, midriff-bared beauties who do several rocking dance numbers and some school cheers, and then combine with their buff male partners for some high-flying acrobatics. I can attest that it really does pump you up, or as players and coaches sometimes put it, gets you "game ready."

As the rally squad departs, calm is momentarily restored and I find myself again being thoroughly fascinated by fan costumes. Walking near me is an old codger with his beard dyed green. Across from where I sit is a middle-aged couple sporting matching Oregon Duck golf shirts. These and much more game-day garb can be purchased in the Duck Shop, which is conveniently located in a corner near the stage, diagonally across from the corner housing the "Order of the O" space reserved for Oregon letter winners. For the moment I find myself focusing on the T-shirts. All manner of Oregon logos and sayings – the usual "Go Ducks" and "Go Big Green," "Hugga Duck," "Get inDuckted," the more esoteric and aggressive "Much the Fuskies" (a reference to the haze of alcohol-aided spelling and hated Pac-10 Conference rival, the University of Washington Huskies), and my personal favourite, "It Never Rains in Autzen." Now anybody even vaguely familiar with Pacific Northwest weather knows that it rains and drizzles often, and the light drizzle that would fall during most of the first half would prove this game day to be no exception. On the same theme, as we finish a second beer and decamp for Autzen Stadium, my cousin points out that the plastic porta-floor under our feet covers artificial turf, the usual groundcover for this expensive, ultra-modern practice facility. The Moshofsky Center serves fans as a Saturday party venue, but it was built as a recruiting lure – a powerful incentive to persuade some of the best golden-tanned high-school players from sunny California that as Ducks, or Webfoots, as they are also known, they would be able

Tailgating: "A Feast of Strangers" • 75

to attend practice inside, safely undercover from the annoying and clammy dampness of the seemingly ever-present Oregon rain.

Inside sold-out Autzen some 58,000 fans are making a lot of noise. We sit behind two fortyish women who are really into it. We get acquainted, and the one wearing UO earrings with a yellow whistle at the ready around her neck reveals that she and her seatmate went to university in Montana. But now their allegiance is to Oregon, where they live, and they are showing it. It was our good luck that neither woman possessed one of those annoying Quackers, an ear-irritating Duck caller, which they might otherwise have used to demonstrate their loyalty.

The spectacle was totally there in front of us – our Montana-transplant neighbours and other rabid fans, the fired-up teams, the band, the rally squad, all the pageantry and colour. But the game itself was a clunker, and while most enjoyed the party and didn't seem to mind, I was unable to take much satisfaction from Duck domination of an obviously weaker opponent. I amused myself watching some fans wearing big-fingered "Go Ducks" mitts and the band's repeated rendition of the school fight song, "Mighty Oregon," while a guy ran across the end zone after each Oregon score waving a huge green flag with a big yellow "O" (think of the biggest U.S. or Canadian flag you've ever seen outside a Husky gas station).

Shortly after the fourth quarter begins we get up and leave the stadium to go check out more of the tailgating scene. We are not alone, because it seems that many other spectators have also departed the game to re-engage with the party that a good many others had apparently never left. Television replaces in-person spectatorship as the party continues at the Moshofsky Center and in the parking lots near the stadium. Among the millions of people who tailgate across America, thousands are not only late for kickoff but do not even bother to enter the stadium. The community they find at the tailgate trumps attendance at the game itself.

Community: From the Crowd That Is Lonely to Togetherness and Conformity

In *The Lonely Crowd*, Riesman, Denney, and Glazer, with their trio of tradition-directed, inner-directed, and other-directed personalities, created types that have since served useful in describing and analyzing social change connecting historical eras and societies. The other-directed theme emphasizing the importance of social acceptance by peers would be taken up a few years later by William H. Whyte in *The Organization Man* (1956) – a figure whom the author discussed at work in the office and at home in suburbia. Whyte's concerns about conformity, and about overconformity, were echoed by many sociologists,[1] artists, and songwriters. My favourite among the songwriters remains socialist activist Malvina Reynolds, whose 1962 song "Little Boxes" critiqued suburban sprawl and the lifestyle that often accompanies it. Her lyrics cover everything from suburban housing ("little boxes made of ticky tacky and they all look just the same") to the university education of the resulting doctors, lawyers, and business executive owners ("they were put in boxes and they all came out just the same"). They cover leisure-time activities ("they all play on the golf course and drink their martinis dry") and the sameness of the culture passed on to the "pretty" children who reproduce it.

The critique of a particular living arrangement does not deny or alter the need that we all have for community, for communal association. Some twenty years after the Reynolds song was written, movie directors John Sayles (*Return of the Secaucus 7*, 1980) and Lawrence Kasdan (*The Big Chill*, 1983) would recall the Woodstock nation by speaking to our need for the togetherness of community in their films. The small screen also speaks to our search for the ties that bind as each year in late January/early February some ninety million viewers gather around their televisions to take in the Super Bowl. This search for community, central to tailgating culture, can also be observed on any and every weekend of the college football season.

Charles R. Frederick's word picture of the community to be found in The Grove at the University of Mississippi (Ole Miss) in Oxford has much in common with the pre-game and post-game celebrations that I observed in Oregon.[2] His description of the Rebel Walk, an event that takes place in a part of the country known for its historic and deep racial divisions, focuses on the sense of community it helps promote between the team, the university, and the school's football fans. The Rebel Walk was started by Billy "Dog" Brewer, who became head coach of the Rebel football team in 1983. According to Frederick, Brewer began the Rebel Walk, a parading event, because he "wanted his players to share in the colorful pre-game atmosphere in The Grove," the university's gathering place – a "10-acre patch of heaven" set amongst thick oak, elm, and magnolia.[3] As Frederick describes it:

> Two hours before the kickoff, Coach Brewer met his team at the athletic dormitory, Kinard Hall, and led them on a leisurely walk through The Grove on their way to Vaught-Hemingway Stadium. The Rebel Walk quickly became very popular with fans. Other teams in the South hold to similar traditions. . . . LSU parades its players through the tailgating throngs and past the mascot Mike the Tiger, who is safely tucked away in his circus wagon cage. At Clemson, the Tigers gather at the top of a hill leading into "Death Valley," where they rub Howard's Rock and race downhill into the Stadium, in what is known as "college football's most exciting twenty-five seconds." . . . As the [Ole Miss] team wends its way through the crowd, many of the fans' comments refer to the physical appearances of the players. I have observed that often the fans, whose usual frame of reference is the uniformed and helmeted player, or a set of height and weight statistics, have little idea about the actual size of the players. The Rebel Walk acts in this way to "humanize" the Ole Miss football team for Rebel fans. It also deepens the connections between the players and their fans. Words of encouragement issued from fans are returned by reassurances from players that they are going to "get after it" later that afternoon. Both players and fans receive an emotional charge from the Rebel Walk.[4]

Denney's term "participative purists," well-suited to the hot-rodders he studied, cannot readily be applied to football tailgaters. Those on hand just for the party or, alternatively, just for the game are relatively few. Most of the participants combine the two in a manner that celebrates a sporting occasion. For the vast majority of tailgaters, activities such as the Rebel Walk offer more than simply the regulation, routinization, and ritualization of fan behaviour; for these are the activities that keep fans from being relegated to the role of passive spectatorship by moving them towards more active participation.

In The Grove at Ole Miss, outside Oregon's Autzen Stadium, at Dartmouth's Memorial Field – in every region of the country – autumn Saturdays mean participation in a festival-like community re-created not only from one weekend to the next but from one generation to the next. In Frederick's South and elsewhere, college football is like religion in that "babies are born into established 'faiths' as fans of particular teams," and as they grow out of their orange and white Volunteer baby booties and red-elephant-inscribed Bama Baby Sleepers they learn and pass on "the deep traditions and values that undergird the festive occasion." In The Grove the enthusiasts are engaging "in a participatory festival." They are not spectators, not simply observers, but active players on the scene. "On Monday morning, if one is asked 'How was The Grove Saturday?' the questioner assumes participation by the respondent. Levels of participation may vary according to age, gender, race, and/or commitment. *But participation is the rule.* No one just watches."[5]

It is, then, a time for community. It is community grounded in family relations and *Habits of the Heart* – a community to replace what Robert Bellah and his collaborators and more recently Robert Putnam argue is often missing in today's American society, where many, according to Putnam, are "bowling alone."[6] One of Frederick's key informants, an Ole Miss graduate and former marching band member who had missed only one home game since 1960, beautifully describes what brings him and his family back to The Grove Saturday after Saturday: "We come here because we are family. We bring the grandchildren because we've got to keep it going."[7]

Lest readers think I am describing a "love-in" marked by the spontaneity of unbridled sociability, I should be clear: there is more to this tailgate-as-community story. It is a regulated community in which behavioural norms are passed on and rules governing proper behaviour (they are posted at The Grove, and on the university's official website) are much in evidence. Tailgating also clearly represents a community marked by class, gender, ethnicity/colour, age, regional, and other divisions and distinctions. It is community that when combined with corporate capitalist direction and class-consciousness and mobility leads

Tailgating: "A Feast of Strangers" • 79

to a social conformity suggested by the other-directedness of *The Lonely Crowd*.

The popularity of sport utility vehicles, one of the transportation modes of choice that I observed on my I-5 trip to Autzen, offers an illustration of both conformity and the search for difference. When compared to cars of the sedan variety, SUVs and their forerunner, Jeeps, have several drawbacks. They are less safe, less fuel-efficient, and more polluting, to name three major problems. And yet, by the turn of the twenty-first century SUVs had become extremely popular among Americans with enough money to afford their relatively expensive but seldom-used off-road capability – even though the vehicles are widely known both for their grievous lack of safety and their environmental hazards.

The rise of SUVs is an almost perfect illustration of the power that can be wielded by a governing class able to bring together big business, government, and labour, all undergirded by military symbolism, in a manner reminiscent of what fifty years ago C. Wright Mills called "the power elite." It is no exaggeration, and in his book *High and Mighty* Keith Bradsher offers a wealth of details to this effect, to say that the SUV domination of the 1990s market turned around a U.S. auto industry under siege by Asian and European imports.[8]

That turnaround, though, may have been short-lived. In late January 2006, Henry Ford's grandson Bill announced a big dip in the venerable company's profits, which would require a remedy of several plant closures and massive layoffs. Slumping SUV sales were highlighted as playing a big part in Ford's retrenchment. It appears that too many Americans are finding not enough rebellion in their Broncos, Explorers, Excursions, Expeditions, and Navigators, and too much conformity. As Heath and Potter demonstrated, "rebel sells." But it is a pseudo-rebellion in which Niedzviecki's "I'm special" feeling gives way to a boring conformity that sends the Lonely Crowd back into the marketplace in search of a new commercialized expression of difference.[9] The corporate-sponsored desire for difference creates product and market differentiation that reproduces, rather than significantly alters, prevailing socio-economic arrangements.

One way of asserting difference is to "do-it-yourself." The recognition and domestication of this modern-day American frontier spirit, as found among do-it-yourselfers, have created some very profitable companies. Home Depot, with its advertising slogan "You can do it, we can help," is an example. So too is the booming tailgate industry. The do-it-yourself spirit characteristic of Denney's "self-sold consumer" is alive, and it is amply promoted by the many prosperous corporations that have a stake in tailgating – which is in itself a study in product diversification.

Corporate Capitalism: Barbecuing and Big Business in the Stadium Parking Lot

Besides the obvious – the development of football as big business at major institutions of higher education – the growth of the tailgate industry involves a wide variety of other business operations. They range from small to megacorporations – from the Big Three automakers and recreational vehicle and gasoline companies to the manufacturers of automobile and truck hitches, lawn chairs, balloons, dining tents, barbeque grills, burger flippers, corkscrews, drinking mugs, tablecloths – the list could go on and on. Indeed, potentially gigantic profits are there to be made in the food and beverage trade alone, market-adjusted and advertised, of course, to take advantage of regional tastes and proclivities.

Whether it is the 60,000 or so who regularly show up at Oregon's Autzen Stadium, or the 80,000 to 100,000 who gather in numerous larger venues across the country, or the 200,000 racing enthusiasts who crowd the track at events sponsored by "NASCAR: A Non-Stop Tailgate Party,"[10] food is a major attraction. Not surprisingly, the vast majority of the more than 1,600 tailgate entries to be found on Amazon.com are items featuring tailgate food and its preparation. And whether the fare is pork or pâté – for class distinctions abound – there is big money for the companies that service the tailgate table.

Research analyzed by the Gale Group showed that 13 per cent of all U.S. consumers had tailgated at least once in the previous year.[11] Tony Miller, spokesman for Hearth, Patio & Barbecue Association (HPBA) notes that with 85 percent of U.S. families barbecuing and 60 per cent of gas-grill owners cooking outside year-round, "there is a big flame to be fanned among tailgaters."[12] In the eyes of grill and car manufacturers, that flame could be big indeed. According to one report, it can be expensive to tailgate in a fashion worthy of "keeping up with the Joneses." Journalist Jason Chow found:

> Tailgating is no longer just a cultural phenomenon. It has become a market segment for makers of vehicles, barbeques and out-door products. Take the Grill-n-Chill, for example. Made by Go Products, the unit attaches to the hitch of an SUV and sports a built-in cooler, a 180-watt CD/MP3 stereo with radio, and, of course, a large grill.
> Price: US$2,495.[13]

For those with deeper pockets who like to arrive early and want to slow-cook, this article suggests they might want to consider the Roadmaster Series of huge trailer-mounted smoker grills made by the Brinkmann Corporation of Dallas, Texas. About eighteen times the size of your standard backyard barbeque, these products retail at anywhere from U.S.$5,500 to $8,000. Or should you desire an all-in-one tailgate vehicle, and you can part with U.S.$70,000, you can order a customized pickup truck from Galpin Motors in California, complete with large grill, two beer keg taps, a blender, and a TV screen. It seats six partygoers. "True success isn't measured in dollars," Galpin president Bert Boeckmann assures his potential clients, "but in the trust of families, friends and customers."[14]

Chow reported that car companies were marketing special "tailgating editions" of SUVs and trucks as well as offering standard features helpful to the tailgater. "The Honda CR-V, for example, has a removable part that unfolds to become a picnic table." In other words, the manufacturers use tailgating to promote SUV sales. "It's now common for a dealer to throw in a tailgating kit, worth as much as US$2,000 to close a deal."[15]

Finally, as Chow noted, corporate America is fast switching from the stadium box seat to the parking lot party, entertaining clients with rented RVs and hired chefs who cook lobsters and steaks to individual preference. On this point he quotes P.J. O'Neil, vice-president of sales and marketing at American Tailgater, a Chicago-based company that specializes in organizing these parking lot events: "Companies are moving away from luxury skyboxes towards the luxury parking spot. It's more fun."

The intense, and competitive, struggle to secure a preferred parking spot is definitely part of tailgate culture, and the HPBA tailgater survey revealed that what most (37 per cent) respondents liked least about tailgating was "traffic and parking hassles." It is the parking hassles, however, that create an opportunity for small business entrepreneurs and charities to make a little money, to cash in on the crumbs that fall off the corporate groaning board.

An article in Eugene's *Register-Guard* (October 15, 2004) reported, for instance, that many Duck fans were leaving the RV-crowded and corporate-bought parking spaces adjoining Autzen Stadium for greener pastures. The newspaper offers an emphatic opinion as to why Autzen's days as "tailgating central" were coming to an end:

> You [Autzen] got too expensive, that's what happened. You sold out to the big donors who pay thousands of bones to park in that big, ugly gravel lot, which is looking more and more like a yacht club social every year. Call us crazy, but we prefer our tailgates to actually have Tail-gates.... The best parties are happening elsewhere, in places such as the BMX track, the Science Factory and the offices of the Boy Scouts of America Oregon Trail Council.... Our favorite ancillary parking lot [and "the best tailgating spot for the non-rich ($20 for cars, $50 for RVs)"] is located right across MLK Boulevard at the Masonic Center, where you'll find footballs flying through the air, hot dogs roasting on open grills and lots and lots of open tailgates. The money goes to charity, and the Masons say they can't remember ever turning anyone away.[16]

Apparently it is at these more distant locations, somewhat remote from the stadium itself, that you can actually find the university's students. A thoroughgoing class analysis might investigate whether parking distance from the stadium, type of tailgate vehicle, and so on correlate with class position. Certainly, parking lot prices dip dramatically as you move further away from the playing field.

The *Register-Guard* article closes with an appeal to the set driving the "65-foot long RV with a satellite TV connection" to come join the party at the Masonic Center.

Tailgating: "A Feast of Strangers" • 83

Here, you can avoid the mad morning rush for an Autzen parking spot – a scene that's been likened to the Oklahoma Land Rush and the Running of the Bulls – by docking your ship the night before. And instead of getting tossed out after the game like yesterday's newspaper (ahem), you can lower the awning, fire up the plasma screen and kick back with a cool one. If you've got an RV, or better yet a decommissioned school bus splashed with green and yellow paint, you can pretty much park all weekend with the Masons. Just imagine: a pre-pre-game party, a pre-game party, a post-game party and post-post-game party.

Make no mistake, to paraphrase the Bard, the party's the thing. It is increasingly common for tailgaters not to interrupt the party by bothering to be present inside the stadium at game time. The HPBA survey discovered that what 65 per cent of tailgaters like most is "time with family and friends." The event itself, the football game, comes in a very weak second, at 20 per cent. Results from another survey reveal that people tailgate for a variety of reasons. Number one is "socializing with friends," which is most important to 71 per cent of those surveyed, while "eating food" comes in a distant second at 13 per cent. Activities like "drinking," "watching the opposite sex," and "being outdoors" were also mentioned, but football, the game itself, did not even register on this list.[17] When American Tailgater organizes a party, game tickets are not part of the typical package of $7,000 to $10,000 that entertains corporate clients in the parking lot.

In short, the live game, like a real vehicle tailgate, is not necessary for the full enjoyment of the sociability of the tailgating moment. In this regard my own medium-sized university of some 7,000 students has evolved beyond most of its sister institutions, demonstrating a trend-setting sophistication that belies its hinterland northern location at the head of Lake Superior. Lakehead University does not field a football team, and we have not only managed to dispense with the game altogether but also learned to concentrate on the main event, the party. What we have somehow managed to set in place is sport as business entertainment without the sporting event: the very definition of both ingenuity and commodification. For instance, on one autumn Saturday afternoon a large crowd gathered to celebrate the successful university hockey team a few days before its season opener. Talking about prospects for the upcoming season and past hockey exploits, celebrants consumed barbecued food and alcohol while negotiating neighbourly stops amidst the SUVs and the many pickup trucks with real tailgates. It was a moveable feast held in the parking lot of a well-known chain steakhouse. With no game – football, hockey, or otherwise – in waiting, and no big-screen TV in sight, the party was the focus. It was an event underlining with clarity the reality that a game was, as we say in the sociology business, neither a necessary nor even a sufficient condition for a tailgate celebration.

Today's tailgater fan may even often feel that game attendance gets in the way of sociability. As Frederick, the chronicler of football Saturdays in The Grove at Ole Miss, observes:

> While football draws thousands to The Grove, some do not even attend the game. The social life is so compelling that football, though the engine for the event, may take a back seat to the festivities around it. One fan I met told me that while he comes to The Grove five or six times a year, he had not been inside the stadium since his undergraduate days. He said: "Why should I leave my friends and this great party, and buy a twenty dollar ticket when I can stay right here and spend two dollars on a Sunday paper tomorrow and read all about the game?"[18]

Professional tailgater Joe Cahn admits he doesn't actually go to the game, only to the game area. Sponsored by a number of corporations, Cahn sold his New Orleans School of Cooking business to hit the tailgate trail. He brought his forty-foot Safari Zanzibar luxury motor home (worth a quarter-million dollars and corporately bestowed by the Monaco Coach Corporation) to Autzen, where parodying an old saw he declared, "It doesn't matter if you win or lose – it's what you eat." Vince Lombardi, the tough-minded, larger-than-life Green Bay Packer coach who, according to legend, declared a half-century earlier that winning was not everything, it was the *only* thing, would not have looked kindly on this point of view. With a camera crew from the Travel Channel documenting his trip, Cahn played down his famous jambalaya and the bottles of personalized spice mix that he was giving away this day. In brief, he de-emphasized the business and social class aspects of his new calling in favour of tailgating's sociability and community elements. Exploring some of the connections between the strange and the familiar characteristic of Denney's work, the self-anointed "Commissioner of Tailgating" compared people back at home, where he says they nervously isolate themselves from strangers with barriers such as privacy fences, caller ID, and e-mail, with the openness of the tailgate party, where "a stranger is just a person you haven't met yet." Pointing to a group of boys at play in the parking lot, Cahn underscored his point. "See that? It's about kids that have a safe place to play," he said. "Tailgating isn't about drinking at 9 in the morning. It's the new party – the new community social."[19]

Class-Consciousness Anew: From Working Class to the Middle and Professional Classes

Just as big business can sponsor and create a corporatized sense of community, so too can social class affiliation. Denney's work, as we've seen, showed a keen awareness of this class element.[20] In his discussion of sports history as social process he emphasized the manner in which ethnic assimilation joined social mobility to promote interaction among social classes, drawing in one instance on the seemingly unlikely pairing of Frederick Winslow Taylor (1856–1915), the founder of industrial management, and coach Walter Camp, the famous (in some circles) "father of football at Yale." Taylor, he said, was "seeking to engender a YMCA morality in a work force increasingly drawn from non-Protestant lands, whereas Camp was inculcating the same morality in young men of undiluted Anglo-Saxon stock and middle-class or upper-class origin." At Yale the footballers spent their summers "as track layers or wheat harvesters in an effort to increase their stamina, moral toughness, and cross-class adventures." In the nearby town of Midvale, home of the American Steel Company, where Taylor was conducting his experiments in motion study and "incentive pay geared to small measurable changes in output," it would be a long time indeed, Denney argued, before the boys of the town would "prove as hard, though fed on kale or spaghetti."[21]

The opportunity to acquire a university education can certainly be viewed as one of these cross-class adventures. Football can lead a recruit to the campus classroom and a class position further up the status ladder of social prestige. Each year the National Collegiate Athletic

Association (NCAA) permits each member school to offer full scholarships to dozens of athletes. Many of these "student-athletes" come from financial and social circumstances that would otherwise make their attendance at university highly unlikely. For these athletes, admission to post-secondary learning promises to open up a new world, and the contacts made, the sociability, may open up yet another new post-school world, regardless of whether or not players leave with a degree in hand. As Denney beautifully summed this up: "For the second-generation boy, with his father's muscles but not his father's motives, football soon became a means to career ascent. So was racketeering, but football gave acceptance too – acceptance into the democratic fraternity of the entertainment world where performance counts and ethnic origin is hardly a handicap."[22] Denney's sense of optimism may well place an outcome burden on democracy that is often unsustainable, but it does capture the potential of football-initiated class mobility.

The other side of the class coin is also worthy of discussion; for just as football can be a class leveller, creating opportunities for class mobility and mixing, it can also reproduce and underscore social class divisions and differences. On-field distinctions abound among players – when, for example, linemen, "the hogs" representing the working class, get down and dirty to protect the stars in the "skill positions" (the quarterback, running backs, and pass receivers), who represent the upper class. Similar distinctions are re-created both in the stands and among tailgaters, before and after the game, starting with whether you drive some kind of vehicle to the game or travel by means of public transportation – and, if you do drive, where you park – and moving from there to how you dress (or costume yourself), what you eat and drink, how you prepare the food and libations, the tailgating equipment you own, all the way to where you sit inside the stadium.

A Day at Dartmouth

A large publicly funded state university such as Oregon offers a great variety in representations of difference and the class distinctions they symbolize. At the Oregon game I noticed, for instance, that the graduate professional and upper classes observed the antics of the working-class "Yahoos" and "Townies" as a source of some amusement. When I went to Homecoming Weekend 2005 at small, privately funded, and prestigious Dartmouth, Denney's alma mater, I saw few "Yahoos" in attendance. I found a scene that was rather different from and provides a contrast to my Oregon experience. It offers lessons in class homogeneity and the governance of class stability.

At Dartmouth order was definitely the order of the day – although admittedly this special well-attended weekend might have been a little more tightly regulated than a normal weekend. I found no list of tailgate rules and regulations to define normative behaviour like the one posted prominently in The Grove at Ole Miss and on the university's official website.[23] Nor did I expect to find that – it would have been too déclassé for Dartmouth. After all, those in the know in and around that institution assume that governing-class gentlemen and ladies know how to behave "properly" and in accordance with their class position. Still, the fraternity, sorority, graduating class, and other parties I observed were well regulated. They were often cordoned off with rope to keep the unwashed and the unwanted out and the select in. Class-consciousness and class affirmation were all too readily observable.

On the Friday evening of Homecoming my wife and I were finishing up dinner at a guidebook-recommended Hanover eatery when lots of noise and band music coming from the street outside made it clear that something was happening out there. Making a hurried exit we found that a crowd had gathered for a passing parade, and apparently we had already missed the first few representatives of graduating classes from years past. Each class marched behind a banner announcing their year of graduation, and sometimes the alumni were accompanied by a decorated vintage automobile. The parade participants represented more than sixty years of alumni history, and we had hit Main Street just in time to catch the class of '56. Eventually the most recent graduates of '05 passed by, followed by first-year students from the class of '09. This last class numbered in the hundreds, around a thousand by my estimate.

The final parade destination for all of the classes was the College Green or Commons area, where Main Street opens up into the Dartmouth campus. I had spent the past three days at the edge of the Commons in the Rauner Special Collections Library working with archival material on Denney. I watched as the frosh class patiently erected a huge, forty-to-fifty-feet-high scaffolding complete with a big '09 at its pinnacle. I was privy to a conversation among library staff members questioning the environmental soundness of using high-grade or building-grade lumber for the Homecoming bonfire. They thought this a waste of precious resources and suggested that older cheaper-grade wood could and should have been recycled for the students' fire. Now I was about to witness this wasted wood spark and smoke up the sky until the '09 top was turned to ashes in the largest and most spectacular fire I had ever seen. Similar Homecoming bonfires and rituals, complete with team introductions and several renditions of the school fight song led by the cheerleading squad, as well as speeches from presidents, distinguished alumni, coaches, and player co-captains, can be observed all over the United States each autumn.

As the gathering of several thousand people watched the four-storey blaze invade the October sky, I could not help but observe my fellow spectators and wonder just who could afford to be here. Each member of the class of '09, now circling the pyramid scaffolding at a dead run – many guys with shirts off and girls clad in skimpy outfits on a night of temperatures at the freezing mark – was paying somewhere between $40,000 to $45,000, and often more, per year for the privilege. Tuition and fees alone for the 2005–06 academic year were billed at $31,965. Estimating non-school-related expenses conservatively, and disregarding tuition and other fee increases plus normal price inflation, the average Dartmouth student could expect her or his four-year education to cost more than *ten* times the amount paid by the average in-state undergraduate at Oregon, where the '05–06 price tag for tuition and fees was $5,853. An Ivy League education costs, though it doubtless has its rewards.

Many of the Dartmouth parents could afford to stay just across from the Commons at the ritzy and exclusive Hampton Inn. In fact, they could observe the goings-on and the bonfire from comfortable chairs on the southern-style front veranda – plantation bosses taking their leisure watching the workers at play? Mothers often sat while their husbands leaned against one of the many Romanesque columns of the open-air porch; sporting deck shoes or fall hiking boots, Docker-style but more expensive casual pants, and colourful blazers with shirt collars open (*sans* ties), they resembled models in *GQ* magazine with a touch of the Lands' End catalogue thrown in. Rooms at the Hampton start at around $300 a night for the smallest, and from there prices climb steadily should you desire more spacious accommodations.

With the fire still adding its orange tinge to the night sky, my wife and I headed away from town towards the many hotels and motels that mark the spot where freeways merge. Our own unHampton-like digs rented at slightly more than $100 for a night's stay. At our motor hotel we found ourselves discussing not only Hanover prices – shops and restaurants seemed only a little more expensive than back home in Thunder Bay – but also something else – something that went beyond the high Hampton rates that permitted only well-paid professionals, physicians and lawyers, perhaps, and well-heeled business people to find each other and a kindred sociability once the shops closed. For us this something is a kind of upper-crust exclusiveness, observable but hard to describe. It is a manner of being in the world that suggests, but certainly never shouts, both "I belong" and "I'm Special," but in a way that is different from what Hal Niedzviecki describes and analyzes.

Dartmouth's Homecoming opponents happened to be staying at our hotel. The members of Columbia's football team looked remarkably similar to my own students back in Canada (baseball hats, shorts, flip-flops, T-shirts and hoodies, earphones and Walkmans/IPods), although on the whole larger. A few exhibited a kind of jock walk or strut common among athletes. During the Saturday morning game-day buffet breakfast, I eavesdropped at a table near some of the players. Their conversations were subdued, befitting the morning hour and that tense time just before the pre-game hype. Their chosen topics – sports, women, music, and an occasional reference to newspaper headlines – were what you might expect at any table of young people, whether they attend university or not. No big debates about the Middle East, no discussions of the second law of thermodynamics, no references either to Noam Chomsky's argument on the deep structure of language or his take on current political controversies. And yet these guys seemed somehow different, and in their manner they let you know it. There was something in the way they carried themselves and in the way they spoke – not what was said but the way in which it was said, their manner of speaking. In the final analysis they were "Ivy League," with all the exclusive specialness the phrase connotes.

At Memorial Field, at the game itself, exclusivity and the reality of being special were even more clearly in evidence. Of course the overall quality of the Ivy League game is different from that played by the most powerful football programs in the country, the difference being not unlike Denney's distinction between amateur and professional.[24] Oregon and other West Coast powers no longer need carry their predecessors' 125-year-old worry that their brand of football does not match up to Ivy League Eastern standards. At the Dartmouth Homecoming the largest cheer, a crowd roar, was reserved not for the quality of particular performances by players, but rather for the five to ten semi-naked students who ran onto the field during the game and were chased down by security officers.

Still, the ritualized outward trappings of the game at Dartmouth resembled those at Oregon in most respects. On hand was the Dartmouth rally squad (with an obviously carefully planned ethnic mix of three whites, three Asians, two blacks, and a Latino), team mascots from both schools, the bands, and students with faces painted in school colours. There was the standard modern and well-lit scoreboard (albeit without the Big Screen or Jumbotron). There were television and radio crews, and the corporate sponsors (local banks and businesses dealing in Toyotas and Unicel phones, as well as the famous Ben & Jerry's ice cream outfit). There were costumed fans of all ages. My favourites among the 6,000-plus onlookers – a much more intimate gathering than the 58,000 at Oregon – were two middle-aged males right out of the "Roaring '20s," complete with full-length "rat tail" brown fur coats topped off by broad-brimmed Jamaican hats (like straw boaters) with Dartmouth-green headbands. For the better part of two quarters my attention kept returning to them. I couldn't help observing how they cheered, properly and not too boisterously, occasionally standing and waving small school pennants. Again something in their manner suggested they were special.

Specialness was clearly on display in the pre-game and halftime activities, when representatives from the visiting school were encouraged to take over the stadium microphone and offer satiric slams of the home institution. It suggested the family-owned business model in comparison to the highly bureaucratized corporate model at Oregon, where it seemed inconceivable that the Autzen microphones would ever be made available for the visiting student body's use. The Homecoming halftime show featured the Columbia band's "All-Star Salute to Mesopotamian Irony." The salute was not only a criticism of the U.S. president's foreign policies, with Columbia's students connecting Iraq with Asian flu; it also set the stage for bringing in animal references and linking them to Dartmouth students and supposed school programs in animal husbandry, a course calendar fiction supplied by the Columbians. The final tune in honor of Avian flu and Dartmouth's probable role in spreading it was entitled, "I Want to Fly Like a Microbe." It was all in good fun. It was good-natured Ivy League joshing, and while I did not find the Dartmouth band's answering material as interesting (perhaps an indicator of the Ivy League's pecking order), the very costume of the band's conductor – he was formally dressed in school-colour white tails and green vest complemented by informal white tennis shoes – may well have been his attempt to poke fun at the Establishment.

Bearing in mind that satire among presumed equals is a form of flattery as well as a demonstration of intelligence, I saw the Homecoming exchanges at Memorial Field as working all so nicely to establish the participants' particular brand of specialness. The football game, for the record won by Dartmouth 17 to 6, is not what is special here; rather it is the general run of Dartmouth and Columbia students, the young and very bright representatives of the prestigious Ivy League known for its elite scholarship, who are special. Unlike Oregon students banished to a Masonic parking lot, Dartmouth students are invited to share centre stage with their on-field colleagues. They are a "we" encouraged to demonstrate through satire their erudite sense of humour, purposefully dismissing the importance and divisiveness of inter-school competition in favour of emphasizing the importance of scholarship over athletics. "We" exhibit the solidarity that unites us in our social class position, regardless of the particular school we have chosen to attend. The pre-game and halftime activities also underscore the Dartmouth reality that only those close to the privileges of power are secure enough, can afford to and are permitted, to poke fun at the establishment without reprisal. At the football field as elsewhere, *we are special*.

But just who is this "we," and how do they mix and mingle? Certainly, at The Grove the oft-cited stereotypic image of middle-aged male tailgaters as Legionnaires loose on the town wearing camouflage outfits and full of beer and bratwursts is represented. But the tailgate party is made up of several social classes and, of course, two sexes. In a humorous review of University of Washington (UW) tailgate partying, *Seattle Times* writer Ron Judd provides a map of who parties where and how.[25] He starts in "The Tyee Lot" at "the very tippy top of the UW tailgate social order, the place where you'll find your boss, U.S. presidents, "the regents, every last one of those darn Nordstroms, retired 26-year-old Microsoft millionaires, caffeine pusher Howard Schultz," and none of "those annoying UW booze patrol rent-a-cops." The gentlemen of the Tyee Lot arrive Thursday morning in a "Motorhome approximately 4 feet longer than downtown Washtucna." They relax over a lunch of "smoked oysters with angel-hair pasta necklaces, Dom Perignon, mussels on half shell and Van de Camp's Fancy-Style Pork'n Brie" while listening to their favourite Neil Diamond tracks. "Honey, don't forget to bring cocktail forks, microwave paper towels and the caterer."

In "Section Two: The Dock" you'll find a floating tailgate party with patrons "whose motorhomes grew so large they eventually were forced to leave the Tyee lot and put out to sea." Here you'll find "lawyers, retired Navy brass, used-car collector Ken Behring, all those darn Weyerhaeusers, your boss's boss." Arrival time is Friday night and the conveyance of choice is a Grand Banks cruiser. For lunch they indulge in "amazing colossal prawns, smoked Snake River chinook salmon, spotted owl'n dumplings and Van de Camp's Pork'n Beluga Caviar," accompanied by masterworks by John Tesh on the sound system. "Honey, don't forget to bring extra deck shoes, universal remote and your personal friend Pete DuPont."

The rest of us, according to Judd – that is, the great majority – are parked in "Section Three: The North Lot, the common man's tailgate venue," where to cut loose with a loud belch is normative behaviour and "half the tailgaters in this section don't even have tickets to the game." Here you'll find "John Keister, your perpetual grad-student brother, victory-starved WSU Cougar fans in purple disguises, 12,000 unemployed former English majors, your boss's lawn boy," but no "golfers, UW faculty – or anyone else in a sweater vest." Arriving in your 1973 Chevy Van just minutes before kickoff, you feast on "Albertson's reduced-fat turkey franks," Pepsi, your choice of several heavily advertised indistinguishable beers and more than one "bigger-than-your-head Costco muffin and Van de Camp's Pork'n Pork'n More Pork" while Jimi Hendrix provides aural excitement. "Honey, don't forget to bring the big blue tarp, duct tape, extra ammo for impromptu Costco-muffin salvos and every one of those damn kids."

Judd's focus upon tailgating difference and class impermeability notwithstanding, there is another point to be made regarding the available space, a few seams and fault lines, in the divisions separating social classes. It is here, especially among the middle and professional classes, that diversity is sometimes tolerated and at least some potential for social-class mixing can be found. For student fans who lack the advancement possibilities provided to their on-field colleagues, the "feast of strangers" offers opportunities for upward social mobility as part of a process that both regulates and reforms distinct class lines. For example, at Ole Miss, a university founded to educate the children of wealthy planters, a place where football is still a dating event, the chance to make both marriageable and job connections means that students "are participating in a large social event with implications for their futures that extend far beyond the final score of the Rebel game," as Frederick notes:

> Ole Miss students often tailgate with their parents in The Grove. Those parents are often members of the state's "ruling class." They are doctors, lawyers, politicians, or business owners; and they tailgate with their friends. Ole Miss students, who move from party to party, meet and socialize with persons who may be potential future employers, investors, or mentors.... What is on the surface a party celebrating college football becomes much more than that. Handshakes, conversation, deportment, etiquette, and sharing food and drink, all may be part of an audition for an unknown role.[26]

The participation of women in this ritual reinforces or reproduces a traditional – in other words, gendered – division of labour, and style. Frederick reports that "women prepare the majority of the food in their home kitchens before Saturday's game," and that they bring the results of "prized recipes" to The Grove.[27] While the red meat dropped on the grills is almost always barbecued by men, it is the women who are "the primary practitioners of the art of frying chicken," the favourite food of tailgating crowds in the South. Women are also heavily involved in the decorative aspect of tailgating. In The Grove it is not unusual to spot silver service and candelabras, and the flower arrangements and tablecloths (sometimes lace) that grace serving tables are handiwork provided by and expected of women. They often serve their food on china, and wear dresses while doing so (the men, according to Frederick, wear jackets). The habits of drinking are, not surprisingly, differentiated. When the women get some time to relax, they often kick back with a lemonade, an iced tea, or a mixed drink; the preferred drinks for women of middle age and older are apparently screwdrivers, bloody Mary's, and mimosas. The men stick with beer and whiskey.[28]

Any analysis of the social and cultural meaning of tailgate parties, then, calls forth the class and gender considerations that underlie and are reproduced by these events. The sociability found among tailgaters does not diminish the importance of the game itself; rather, the sociability makes the game even more important, more socially significant, as the Lonely Crowd reaffirms not only the fellowship to be found on each rung of the social ladder but also the potential web of relationships to be constructed between the rungs. As Denney made clear in his study of "The Leisure Society," we often might wonder, as play and work are transformed into each other, or one another, whether we are being used by leisure. Our musings aside, we remain social animals who – while we make sure to secure our own ground – enjoy participating in the feast, rubbing shoulders both with class familiar and, sometimes, class stranger.

CHAPTER 6

The Fourth Quarter

Higher Education Joins the Party

HIGHER EDUCATION IS BIG BUSINESS. Often the university is the major employer or one of the most important employers in a city. For students, university has become a kind of Mecca. Better than 50 per cent (some U.S. observers report 70 per cent) of college-age Americans and Canadians begin some sort of post-secondary education, with half of these obtaining a university undergraduate degree. Today's university has become the training ground for employment that the high school was sixty to seventy years ago.

The university is, however, both a place and an experience that encompasses more than simply job preparation. University students, like the rest of us, are in search of a kind of sociability that, in Ray Oldenburg's words, is "disappearing for want of settings" that make it possible.[1] The subtitle of Oldenburg's book *The Great Good Place* lists a number of those potential settings: "cafes, coffee shops, bookstores, bars, hair salons, and other hangouts at the heart of a community." To that list I would add the university as a place that many people, young and old, seek out to counter a suburbia- and television-created isolation – and, of course, a university, often complete nowadays with its own shopping mall, contains all of the features that Oldenburg lists, right down to the hair salon. "We glorify our freedom *not* to associate," Oldenburg says, referring to this standardized isolation. "The problem of place in America manifests itself in a sorely deficient informal public life. The structure of shared experience beyond that offered by family, job, and passive consumerism is small and dwindling."[2]

Oldenburg's solution is to encourage the search for and development of "third places" that would balance daily life found in the two realms of domestic and job experience with a third, more inclusively social and different, kind of experience. I would suggest that university as a place and experience is part of this search, although I am admittedly dubious, not sanguine, about the sociability to be found among those engaged in what Veblen critiqued nearly a century ago as *The Higher Learning in America*. Again, for me, Denney's comments on youth and sociability provide a road map into this tricky territory.

The sociability to be found in today's higher education is typified in the corporate branding of universities. Advertising that brings both increased profits and higher student enrolments provides an all-too-perfect fit with the "beer and circus" world of big-time intercollegiate sports and tailgate partying. The result is an emphasis on the sociability of the party at the expense of the sociable necessities and possibilities of scholarly engagement. A commodified higher education, complete with school rankings, performance indicators, and specialized training in the professions serves to create a rather homogenized student body in which the search for a third place becomes the party. The party becomes a way in which students can combat the anxiety of the Lonely Crowd and maybe even find a special niche that allows them to stand apart from the crowd by highlighting their individual uniqueness. Of course, this search for "the great good place," the party place, is, as always, underwritten and sustained by the social class relations of the society at large.

The Classroom as Edutainment Joins Football as Entertainment

As Riesman and Denney noted, football as it developed in the United States was different from early British football in its class orientation and participation.[3] The different developmental paths turned upon a difference between class aristocracy and movement towards a more egalitarian class system. Riesman and Denney contended that Americans were not willing to subordinate themselves to a collegiate aristocracy in the same "gentlemen's" manner as were their British counterparts. The cultural requirements and changing performance standards of the American game extended participation downwards in the class structure – so much so, for instance, that in the 1890s, in a time of ethnic diversity on the field, and when arguments with the referee occurred as a matter of routine after most plays, a good linguist was a prized asset for the team.[4] Today, of course, recruiting a linguist is no longer a top priority of big-time (or the less-well-known) college football programs. Sports recruiting has changed in a manner that corresponds with, and has helped create, current techniques and standards governing academic recruitment.

American higher education, like the football programs it sponsors, is part of a growing and profitable entertainment industry. Indeed, in the United States it is often the football programs that are sponsoring higher education. Not just sponsoring: according to Murray Sperber, in his book *Beer and Circus*, big-time sports is also *crippling* undergraduate education. In researching his book Sperber sent out a questionnaire to universities across the country asking questions such as "How important a factor in your decision to attend your university was the fame of the school's intercollegiate athletic teams?" and how important was "the fame of the school's party scene connected to its college sports events?" The results revealed an important split between schools in the National Collegiate Athletic Association's Division I, which award athletic scholarships, and schools in Division III, which do not. In Division I schools, large percentages of respondents responded affirmatively when asked if their choice of college had something to do with athletics and partying. At the NCAA Division I schools, in the answers to both questions asked, some 56 per cent of males considered both of the factors to be "very important" or "moderately important." Some 31 per cent said they were "neither important or unimportant," and 13 per cent said they were "moderately unimportant" or "very unimportant." The young women at the schools answered much less enthusiastically: 26 percent were positive, 38 percent neutral, and 36 percent were negative. Significantly, though, Sperber found that the undergraduate students at Division III schools "recorded numbers that almost reversed the Division I males."[5]

The University of Oregon, the site of our tailgating adventure – and a place that exemplifies strong football-academic connections – was one of the universities that Sperber investigated. According to Sperber, UO offers a near-perfect sports marketing success story. Many UO students responded in the affirmative to Sperber's athletic-team and party questions, a finding that goes well beyond high rankings on various "party school" lists and the attempts of beer-drinking fraternity students to make campus reality resemble scenes from *National Lampoon's Animal House* (1978), the John Belushi movie filmed on the Oregon campus. It also hides the diversity of the Oregon student body, where beer-loving fraternity brothers and sorority sisters sit in class alongside "independents," non-drinkers, liberal vegetarians, tree-hugging environmentalists, business majors of a conservative bent, joggers, and famous runners, among others.

During the 1970s and 1980s varsity athletics at the University of Oregon were not unimportant, but even those undergraduates who were paying close attention to sports seemed to accept the university's almost perennial position near the bottom of the Pacific-10 standings in football and basketball. By the late 1980s, though, state and federal cutbacks to higher education combined with university athletic budgets that routinely ran large deficits had created a financial crisis at Oregon. There were hearty proposals in the state legislature and considerable faculty agitation to cut athletic funding and Pac-10 ties.

Then, enter a new UO president. Myles Brand assumed the post in 1989, and Brand had a plan that over the next few years not only restored financial order at the university but also rewarded him with a 1994 appointment as president of Indiana University and later, in 2003, the prestige and security of the presidency of the NCAA. The Brand plan to solve Oregon's financial woes involved strong administrative encouragement for an upgrade of the school's athletics program; it flew directly in the face of the proposals to cut back and break the Pac-10 ties. Brand argued that Pac-10 membership was essential to the university's recruitment drive, and according to Sperber "he tenaciously fought the proposal to deemphasize" the school's sports program. Brand went out and raised money for the football team from a variety of new sources. One faculty member remarked that the president "can work the alums at a football game as well as anybody."[6]

Oregon teams thereafter became more successful. The football team finally got to a bowl game after a twenty-five-year absence and won the Pac-10 conference championship and played in the 1995 Rose Bowl. In the end President Brand's patient adherence to his planned strategy of aggressively marketing sports resulted in the development of a sports-party image that paid dividends. Brand in effect "branded" the University of Oregon. He "repositioned" the school as being more "student friendly" – aided by the admissions office's help in putting a positive spin on the university's "Animal House" connections.

Brand's approach had some fortunate help from conditions in the neighbouring state of California, where a financial crisis had led to decreased funding for public colleges and universities. Oregon promised "a more collegiate atmosphere" than did the deteriorating California institutions, and the result was an increasing number of entering freshmen coming to the school from out of state, most of them from California suburbia. These students willingly paid high out-of-state tuition fees – three times more than the in-state fees – just to buy into the Oregon atmosphere. After Oregon appeared in the Rose Bowl, the applications for tuition jumped by another 20 per cent – again with out-of-state applicants making up the largest percentage of the new cohort.[7] Sperber sums up the experience:

> The Oregon admissions saga was somewhat unusual – part of its success connected to a financial crisis in a nearby state with a huge population – but this university was also typical of schools that found Enrollment Valhalla in the 1980s and 1990s by emphasizing beer-and-circus. . . .
>
> In the mid-1990s, when the "baby boomlet" (the children of the baby boomers) entered higher education, enrollment numbers improved, but at many Big-time U's, the lessons learned during the down period of the previous fifteen years – market the hell out of college sports and the festivities surrounding it – were ingrained and continued into the twenty-first century.[8]

President Brand's brand has stuck. Even though Oregon has not risen to the great heights of the top twenty "party schools" on the famous annual *Princeton Review* and likewise did not make it onto the list of ten schools on the 2006 *Playboy* list, its reputation as a fun place remains intact. To retain some of the image without being listed as a top party campus is probably better for the academic image. The rise of football power University of Texas to party prominence resulted in that school's support of the American Medical Association's call for an end to the "party school" list. The AMA stated that "the rankings promote the notion that excessive drinking is the college norm."⁹

Google "student drinking," and you will find a wealth of material showing that physicians are not the only ones worried about campus drinking. They are joined by addiction researchers and counsellors, social workers, psychologists, sociologists, and various youth observers – and of course concerned parents and students themselves. Many research studies, past and ongoing, show that drinking among college students is undoubtedly widespread, with about 80 per cent of students reporting that they imbibe, and a significant number of these, around 40 per cent, say they drink five or six times a month, downing four to six drinks on each occasion. Factors such as gender (women drink less often and less than men), age (older drink more than younger), region, and legality also enter into the experience. Binge or high-risk drinking is a major concern, and university-sponsored programs and forums that encourage responsible alcohol use are plentiful. The responsibility message seems to be getting through, and slightly more than 20 per cent of all students now report that they do not use alcohol at all.

Whether they use alcohol or abstain, students, just like their tailgating parents and alumni, want to preserve as many long weekends as possible. Students not surprisingly have a high regard for the three-day weekend – many of them tailor their timetables, that is, their choice of courses, to achieve this effect – and are strongly opposed to attempts by several campus administrations to "reclaim" Fridays for classroom, or scholarly, activities. It seems that some university authorities want to increase the total number of classes offered on that day, as well as support more sessions with early morning start times.[10]

The administrators' objective seems to follow the theory that university life should at least approximate "real life" after schooling. The culture of heavy partying rather than studying on Thursday nights seems to be an administrative sore point, but then too, as an article in the UO student newspaper points out, a significant number of students use their long weekends to catch up on reading and to complete essays and other long-term class projects. In any case, the student journalist adds, "It is not the responsibility of a university to regulate the social life or social [and potential work] schedule of students." Then too, in the "real-life" world of gainful employment after graduation, partying may well serve up about the same percentage of hangovers, missed work, and falling behind at work as college partying did, for instance, at Pennsylvania State University, where drinking left 59.8 per cent of the students with hangovers, caused 25.9 per cent of them to miss a class, and 20.7 per cent to fall behind in their school work.[11]

Sociability facilitated by the bottle certainly transcends College Park (Penn State), Eugene, or any other town or campus. Indiana University student John Blevins reported on a semester that he spent in Spain at the Universidad de Sevilla – and that he spent it drinking with other U.S. college students from Penn State, Oregon, Clemson, Florida State, and Ohio State, which relieved his worry that "I wouldn't fit in."[12] Blevins was able to bridge any troublesome cultural gaps by making Seville, Cordoba, and Granada outposts of Bloomington, Indiana, complete with a discovery of "this great bar" near the Sevilla campus "where they've got Dave Matthews on the jukebox and Sam Adams on tap" – in other words, an "American bar" on Spanish soil.

The satisfying experiences of student-abroad Blevins and what many consider the value in President Brand's Oregon brand are joined and reach their apogee in the party. These experiences offer a seamless transition easing the student journey from campus community to the community at large. This point is crucial in understanding both tailgate-party behaviour and the place of an undergraduate education in the lives of students. Tailgating, like the designation "student," creates particular anxieties, but for many it also brings welcome relief from the general anxiety of other-direction, the feeling that one is "at home everywhere and nowhere." The search for Oldenburg's third place is made less stressful, at least during football season. Students can even add basketball and perhaps another sport to have the academic year, if not the calendar year, well covered. All they have to do is simply renew their membership in tailgate culture and then party on! Tailgating may not be a life goal, but the tailgate party and the sociability that goes with it extend higher education as a less-than-scholarly lifestyle beyond graduation, transcending the peculiarities of cultural and subcultural difference to become a lifestyle for life.

The Crowd Becomes Less Lonely: The Consumerist Model and University Training

A seamless fit between campus and the larger community explains and goes beyond the Portland Brewers truck and its advertised mission to bring "Beer To The Game" in Eugene and elsewhere. The fit speaks to a statement that Denney made about the transition from youth to adult being centred on money and markets: "Perhaps it is more a matter of the purse than anything else. The twelve-year-old suburban girl whose shopping list read 'water-pistol, brassiere, and permanent' was demonstrating not merely the tremors of transition but also purchasing power. If you can buy as an adult, you *are* an adult."[13]

Justification for the money spent by governments, corporations, alumni, parents, and students on today's higher education comes at a time when critics are emphasizing the massive collection of statistics that provide measures of "accountability" – for example, measuring "throughput," or how quickly students can move through degree programs. "The growing popularity of rankings," Canadian analyst William Bruneau notes, has "coincided with a mini-revolution in government policy, the appearance of so-called performance indicators." Arguing that "American and Canadian experiences of ranking have many similarities," Bruneau points out:

> Rankings and performance indicators on both sides of the border are strongly influential in public funding and governance decisions. This is big "business," tied closely to the appearance of Thatcherist and Reaganite schemes of government micro-management, and combined over the past 30 years with sharp cuts in public funding for higher education.[14]

This kind of attention, and strict guidance, leads to governance by market measures, to a situation in which any hint of university autonomy becomes a wish not to be fulfilled and expressions of educational quality are forced into a consumerist mould. The reputational rankings that often count most in the minds of students can be found in the weekly Associated Press list of the top twenty-five U.S. college football teams and the *Princeton Review* list of the country's top party schools. As Twitchell documents, schools are in a feverish, fun competition with one another to increase their enrolments:

So the University of Houston has a $53 million wellness center with a five-story climbing wall. Washington State University has the largest Jacuzzi on the West Coast (it holds fifty-three students), Ohio State is building a $140 million complex featuring batting cages, rope courses, and the now-necessary climbing wall, and Southern Mississippi is planning a full-fledged water park.[15]

On-campus fun centres and the proximity to a campus of fun beer halls and exciting nightclubs (don't forget karaoke) manufacture a kind of consumer consent that trumps the classroom work of the scholars, distinguished and otherwise, who fill the ranks of academia.

That consumerism, Denney's "matter of the purse," would govern higher education's development is no big surprise to anyone who has studied the many economic connections between the growth of U.S. colleges and universities and the structure of the larger economy.[16] Since at least the early nineteenth century, higher education and business have had a tight connection. In a process that reflects what I think of as "the death of the sensible," universities have altered their shape to accord with and to accommodate the changing needs of the very same socio-economic system that dominates their continued maintenance and development; and the transformation of university curriculums from a classical to a more practical, vocational orientation has been a key to this accommodation.[17]

Today the educational system's orientation emphasizes an extended period of formal schooling as preparation for full-time work. It is this extended socialization in schools, modelled after and reproducing prevailing socio-economic arrangements, that creates the twin phenomena that Neil Postman, in his book *The Disappearance of Childhood* (1982), identified as the adult-child and the child-adult, a transformation of the lonely crowd's anxiety into consumerism. Denney, anticipating Postman by twenty years, elaborated on the resulting homogeneity in his suggestion that young people had become "rather more like each other than they have been since the Civil War."[18] The cookie-cutter sameness characterized in the Malvina Reynolds song stifles meaningful dissent in favour of consumerism. "The age of extended socialization is in full swing," Denney wrote in 1962.

> One of the odd effects of extended socialization is that it seems to us older ones to be connected as much with a downward extension of age-graded roles and a general widening of privileges as it does with the postponement of a full career as an adult. . . . It has also been said . . . that one reason the young in the United States do not organize themselves as a social and political movement is that they are already organized by our society as a body of affluent consumers.[19]

Admittedly, since these words were written significant changes have occurred, especially the organization of several student movements. But the organized body of young consumers remains.

It is a generalized allegiance to a consumerist model that has produced "the shopping mall high school," which is the title of a book written more than twenty years ago by Arthur G. Powell, Eleanor Farrar, and David K. Cohen.[20] These authors describe a mind-boggling array of between four and five hundred proffered courses. This "something for everybody" variety that had become characteristic of metropolitan high schools is also to be found in post-secondary schooling, where "the elective has become the core curriculum"[21] Powell, Farrar, and Cohen note a four-hundred-credit course catalogue that "resembled those of large colleges." They saw another school catalogue that looked like a newspaper advertising supplement. Some thirty-six large (eleven by seventeen inches) pages of newsprint "were required to explain 480 courses and other educational services." This surfeit of courses, like the expanding number of professionalized disciplines and integrated fields characterizing today's multi-campus multiversities, appears to be an ideal variegated model, a perfect smorgasbord of do-it-yourself options for creating a personalized field of study. This represents the business-oriented vocationalized model of university education, or maybe we should call it the tailgate model. For what appears to be lots of choice and variety, upon closer inspection reveals a hidden dumbed-down curriculum emphasizing a kind of sociability reminiscent of the party atmosphere at a beery football tailgate.

In all of this the students are primarily the victims and should not shoulder too much of the blame for the continuing curriculum inadequacies. Many students do express a firm desire to work in a more scholarly environment, but the university-as-job-training emphasis tends to undermine that goal. The general tendency, I fear, is to acquiesce in support of a one-dimensional, tailgate curriculum. Sociability replaces the tough standards of the more rigorous and supposedly less differentiated curriculum – there were not enough options, it was said – that was lost when universities jettisoned classical studies in favour of modern or postmodern menus. This curriculum conflict goes well back in time. The staples of classical studies – rhetoric, the languages and literary works of Latin and Greek origin, philosophy, mathematics – were, for instance, the rallying point of Yale University faculty members in a document known as "The Yale Report of 1828," which argued against a collegiate education that looked only to the practicalities of the present moment (vocationalism) and in favour of laying foundations for a "superior education." As the report put it, "The two great points to be gained in intellectual culture, are the discipline and the furniture of the mind; expanding its powers and storing it with knowledge."[22]

Perhaps not all that much has changed since 1828. The culture of tailgating fits neatly into what has become today's standard: the differential marketing of education. It is an integral part of what John Taylor Gatto has analyzed as "dumbing us down."[23] Denney wrote about the roots of this same tendency as early as 1962. The exact statistic on the reading of books might have changed – perhaps for the worse? They have the Internet, and who needs books? – but the issue remains:

> The educational preparation of the young poses three issues of great importance that are troubling us now: inequality of opportunity, premature specialization, and the glorification of the average. . . . American higher education presents a widely mixed scene in which vocationalism still runs strong. More students take degrees in business than in either the sciences or humanities and the average college student in the United States is culturally illiterate. More than half of them, for example, read less than seven books a year.[24]

In another essay written two years later Denney was still remarking on the dangers of this trend: "I myself do not see how the health of the American college and university can be maintained in the face of a vocationalism that is both persistent and narrow."[25]

Many a student dream is compromised by early school and university socialization. Denney's comments on the new world of bureaucratized professionalism facing the youth of 1960 were prescient in suggesting the kind of university education that has continued to be developed and refined in the years since he wrote:

> Youth lives in a world in which physical action and labor have been replaced by brain work and in which clean-cut personal goals are less evident than the subdivided, bureaucratic adjustments to role.... With the decline of status associated with class and family the vacuum has been filled by status associated with the professional badge.[26]

The limitations of professional schooling are nicely captured in a book written by physicist and former graduate student Jeff Schmidt, who took "a critical look at salaried professionals and the soul-battering system that shapes their lives," which is the subtitle of his book *Disciplined Minds*.[27] Like Schmidt, I argue that the addiction of students to authority and standardization is promoted by their schooling, which teaches them to discipline academic and job content to a professionalized form. Learning and relearning the lessons of professional submission are both a kind of reductionism and social control, useful in reinforcing the complementarity of the professional and academic hierarchies that sustain the corporate system that shapes students. In the commodification of education students are bought and taught to buy into the system in a manner that is both unimaginative and non-threatening – which, from the perspective of most potential employers, is a bonus.

Historian David Noble makes a useful distinction between training and education – a distinction that informs my critique and Schmidt's as well:

> In essence, training involves the honing of a person's mind so that his or her mind can be used for the purposes of someone other than that person. Training thus typically entails a radical divorce between knowledge and the self. Here knowledge is usually defined as a set of skills or a body of information designed to be put to use, to become operational, only in a context determined by someone other than the trained person;

in this context the assertion of self is not only counterproductive, it is subversive to the enterprise. Education is the exact opposite of training in that it entails not the disassociation but the utter integration of knowledge and the self, in a word, self-knowledge. Here knowledge is defined by and, in turn, helps to define, the self. Knowledge and the knowledgeable person are basically inseparable.[28]

Noble emphasizes that the process of education is interpersonal and "not merely interactive." He mentions that what people tend to recall about their educational experiences is "above all not courses or subjects or the information imparted but people, people who changed their minds or their lives, people who made a difference in their developing sense of themselves . . . the relationship between people is central to the educational experience." What education is all about is "the establishment and enrichment of this relationship" – the "process of becoming for all parties, based upon mutual recognition and validation and centering upon the formation and evolution of identity." That is the "actual content of the educational experience."

Given the prevailing type of university education, in which the potential sociability of scholarship is turned into specialized training, a division of labour that Denney "felt to be reaching almost into the kindergarten,"[29] is it any wonder that many students live for the party? The situation Denney described nearly half a century ago has only gotten worse: "Industrial practices, professional restrictions, educational prerequisites often seen to have much more to do with the elaboration of specialized job functions than do the requirements of the job themselves."[30] When one is, in Paul Goodman's words, "growing up absurd," to "party on" makes a lot of sense.

Fun and Games at the University: Higher Education as Style for Life

In the United States the issues related to job overqualification and its connection to technological change have been recognized since the 1970s, when Eugene S. Schwartz wrote about overskill and the decline of technology in modern civilization and Richard B. Freeman argued that Americans were overeducated for what was required to do the jobs available to them. In Canada in the late 1990s, D.W. Livingstone's work on the education-jobs gap provided data regarding the lack of fit between limited and limiting job requirements and the wealth of knowledge possessed by Canadian workers.³¹ The boredom resulting from job overqualification is not far removed from the boredom that many students face in the classroom. Indeed, the issue of school boredom can be traced through the connections between formal education, student apathy and hostility, and the effects of compulsory school as a legal obligation.³²

The party can be an excellent antidote for both the tedium of job overqualification and school boredom. As Denney also pointed out, "A good many of the activities of the young, including their high-school and college courses, are preparations for leisure."³³ Perhaps Denney was anticipating, and might even have been sympathetic to, one of Sperber's sports-fan respondents who in the P.S. section of his completed questionnaire wrote, perhaps tongue-in-cheek (but who knows?), "I always dreamed of wearing purple and gold [Louisiana State's colours] in college, and majoring in tailgating. I'm glad I fulfilled my dream."³⁴

Boredom at school begins early, and for students caught in "the rat race" of becoming professionalized so too does the search for Oldenburg's third place – a place that offers some sociable freedom from the other two realms of labour force and domestic experience. Today's third place is often a moveable feast of friends and sometimes strangers, typified by the tailgate party. In contrast to the lyrics sung by the 1970s and 1980s football broadcaster Don Meredith, "Turn out the lights, the party's over," his way of indicating that the outcome of a particular game was no longer in doubt – for many tailgaters the party rages on long after the stadium lights are doused.

Well before the last tailgate is folded up, a growing number of college students are already putting down wagers against next Saturday's betting lines. Student gambling has become a widespread problem, with disheartening outcomes. In the world outside the university, recent Super Bowl XL bettors wagered on everything from the time of kickoff to firsts with regard to fumbles, interceptions, passing and running touchdowns, penalties, and much more, plus the usual bets on point spreads, total points scored, and even the traditional who-will-win. In 1999, for instance, research at the Harvard University Medical School Division was showing that "more youth are introduced to gambling through sports betting than through any other form of gambling activity."[35] The students' connection to the culture surrounding the campus, including the gambling culture, is clear, and so too is gambling's connection with alcohol use among students.[36]

You also do not have to be a gambler to enjoy the party that joins gaming with alcohol. Point-spread knowledge is not necessary in the many college drinking games that invite participation. Drinking games are often connected to viewing television programs favoured by students.[37] One game I became familiar with is based on the popular Fox network series *The O.C.* ("The Orange County"). The main characters in the program come from neighbouring families in the ritzy surroundings of Newport Beach, California. The adults have both high-octane jobs and social lives, as do their teenage kids and significant others; and the youth, with allowance for the usual generational spats, model themselves after their parents. Both family hardships and successes are monitored by plenty of money and warm California sunshine conducive to "beautiful people" enjoying a party lifestyle.

The game, according to The OC website,[38] involves the participants taking a drink whenever they observe certain behaviours among the "regular occurrences" on the program, and in particular those involving the four young stars. Ryan's patented sideways look, leggy girlfriend Marissa in a miniskirt, Seth's teenage angst displayed in a derogatory reference to himself, and girlfriend Summer's oft-repeated "ewwwwww" are all worth a drink. In the case of "hopeless loser" Seth, it's worth two drinks. Some occurrences – "the big ones" – are worth even more: three drinks every time "someone from Ryan's past makes an appearance," five drinks for "same-sex smut." Players are simply advised to "pound your beer" whenever a "character loses his/her virginity." A ten-drink – "minimum kegstand" (read well on the way to oblivion) – is required whenever a cast member from the show's ancestor drama *Beverly Hills 90210* makes an appearance.

One Thursday evening I was invited (allowed?) to participate in and observe "the O.C. night" with my nineteen-year-old, university-student daughter and some of her friends. Drinking was moderate – perhaps more so because I was there – but I did learn that, at least in this group, a drink can mean a sip for those not wanting to get drunk, and I was told that non-alcoholic drinks are respected for those who want not to imbibe. I also learned that Seth's cynicism in no way made him a loser; every young woman in attendance thought he was "hot" and dreamed of spending time with someone so adorably witty. We all had lots of fun. Maybe Steven Johnson is right in his treatment of pop culture as becoming increasingly sophisticated because it seems as if "everything bad is good for you."[39] Keep the TV lit, throw back a tall cool one, and party on!

Sports gaming is also big among the college crowd. In his celebration of the release of the pro football video game "Madden 2004," Chris Suellentrop charts John Madden's popularity as a broadcaster, former NFL coach, and producer of a video game that has made this personality into "the new Nike, sport's official arbiter of cool." Suellentrop notes that the Pro Football Hall of Fame in Canton, Ohio, "decided that America's best-selling sports game merited its own 300-square-foot display." To be the cover boy on the annual reissue of the Madden game is "a career-defining experience, the way an enormous shoe contract, or the Wheaties box, or the cover of *Sports Illustrated* once determined which sports stars had hit the big time."[40]

Console gaming, not the personal-computer gaming of the geeks, with Madden on the PlayStation, Xbox, or GameCube, "has become a staple of dorm rooms and locker rooms alike." Madden outsells everything but the Grand Theft Auto games. Why? Suellentrop speculates that a good measure of Madden's popularity is "due to the strength of the product: It's an action game, a role-playing game, and a serious stimulation, all in one." It's a learning experience that Felix Gillette, in his testimonial on the virtues of "Madden 07," argues that television could learn from "by throwing a few Madden flourishes into their coverage" – more use of the SkyCam, graphics noting the substitutions on both offence and defence before the play begins, and after the play "quickly flash a Madden-esque graphic with multicolored vectors depicting the routes that the receivers just ran across the field."[41]

Here we have education without the classroom – an "edutainment" with the kind of holding power that most lectures and textbooks lack. Or, borrowing the colourful analogue employed by a vice-president of EA Sports, the Madden game's publisher, in describing Madden and the sports video-game industry as a whole: "We're sort of a direct competitor to girlfriends."[42] This is an awareness that my O.C. game-playing daughter and her friends may or may not share.

Denney's concerns for the youth of the 1960s are still with us.[43] In the education of today's young, "inequality of opportunity, premature specialization, and the glorification of the average" continue to trouble us. The sociability of both sport and the party speaks to all three of these issues. Success at partying connects youth with their peers in a way that makes the crowd less lonely. In the same moment, as was the case for Sperber's P.S. respondent dreaming of a tailgate major, it also offers opportunities to create an "I'm Special" niche or possibly even to rebel – all within the acceptable limits laid down by consumerist culture, of course.[44] What university attendance comes down to for many students is more than the years of training in a professional specialty that leads to a good job or the gathering of potential mates (suggested by the proverbial and out-of-date MRS degree) headed for domestic bliss. It is essentially Oldenburg's search for a sociable third place – a *Cheers* beyond home and work, a place "where everybody knows your name."

CHAPTER

Overtime

Distance Education, Sociability, and the Song of the Sirens

> It has been a pleasant risk to try to assign meanings to the plural myth of the popular culture of the moment. To suggest what the future holds, other than a decline of the naïvely realistic, would be difficult. It is easier to show what astonished the muses yesterday than to say what song the sirens will sing tomorrow.
> – Denney, *The Astonished Muse*, p.253

IN 1964 DENNEY DELIVERED A CONFERENCE PAPER that considered the "dialogue between age and youth" of the day – the 1960s were, after all, the time when the term "generation gap" came into vogue as a loose description of the cultural differences between the baby boomers and their parents. In particular the paper looked at students and their part-time and summer employments in a growing service economy. "This youthful work economy is not," he wrote, "by and large, vocationally directed, even though it may serve as a way of trying out possible occupations. It is rather a form of paid sociability combined with study, an existence in which the student-waiter brings some of the campus to the resort and uses the pool after hours."[1] His idea of employment as "a form of paid sociability combined with study" anticipated today's widespread acceptance of "life-long learning." He noted that while these work activities "involve job-holding," they "do not involve a vocational aim but a general educational aim. The job and the job skill are not the aim; they are the means by which the young person 'gets around' and engages in a form of self-education that he cannot get in any other way."[2] Of course, in more recent years the aim

• 115

of many students of middle-class and working-class backgrounds is also definitely income – gaining the money necessary to pay off rapidly escalating tuition fees and expenses.

In the paper Denney also pondered the shape of life at the other end of the age continuum. "In western society, time comes from the future," he said, suggesting that in older traditional societies it "comes from the past." Time is thus "sweeping past the Now of mankind into the historical." This leads "to the paradoxical concession that the old can learn from the young and even that, in times of rapid technical and cultural change, the old *have* to learn from the young."[3] Again, Denney's observations anticipate the movement towards "life-long learning."

Denney argued against the "training" emphasis that he saw as so often characterizing school learning and in favour of a more "liberal," maybe even somewhat "classical" curriculum. Given that "the labors of a working life have been lessened and the extent of biological life has been lengthened," he asks, "is it possible to use these perceptions to provide an education up to the age say of eighteen which is less specialized in the vocational sense in order that a base may be provided for the growth possibilities of the later ages?" He quickly answered that question by arguing that educational opportunities for both young and old were being extended through the young's service employment: "this new juvenile 'right to be philanthropic' as one kind of the general educational processes which has true depth of possibility as an education for later stages of life."[4]

For Denney, then, service to and sociability with others were central to the growth possibilities in learning over the life cycle. Again, Denney was prescient in anticipating another of today's social movements, volunteering. He describes it as a giving of oneself reminiscent of the elite's philanthropic activities, but it is also a giving that is open to a much broader cross-section of the population – it is the volunteer movement as a kind of democratized sociability.

Denney, Simmel, and McLuhan on Sociability, Technology, and Learning

Sociability as education, or as learning in its broadest sense, was a frequent theme in Denney's writings and, not surprisingly, was also a prominent theme in the work of one of his mentors, Georg Simmel.

Simmel (1858–1918), the youngest of seven children, was born into a prosperous Jewish family in Berlin. He was a contemporary of Emile Durkheim (1858–1917) and Max Weber (1864–1920), two thinkers who, along with Karl Marx (1818–83), "had a significant influence on the development of modern sociology."[5] But Simmel's scholarly career took a decidedly different path from theirs as he remained mostly an outsider both to the academy and the discipline of sociology. Yet Simmel may have been the first academic in Germany to offer a course in sociology, which he did at the University of Berlin, and by the middle 1890s he was becoming well known outside Germany. The Durkheim-edited journal *L'Année sociologique*, for instance, published a Simmel essay in its first issue in 1896; and, as his biographer David Frisby points out, "Between 1896 and 1910 no fewer than nine of Simmel's sociological essays, largely due to the initiative of Albion Small, appeared in the newly established *American Journal of Sociology*."[6] Simmel and his wife, Gertrud, herself a philosopher, were close to the leading artistic figures at the heart of the cultural and artistic scene in Germany and elsewhere. Active in several working groups of Berlin intellectuals in the late nineteenth and early twentieth centuries, Simmel practised the sociability he wrote about, hosting a salon that met weekly in his home.

In his writings on culture Simmel explored the subjects of sociability in general (*sociation*), play, leisure, transportation, communication, work, and even architecture. For example, in his essay "The Alpine Journey" he wrote about the effects of the new railway line into the Alps, of the cultural change brought about by this mass transportation: "It is something more than an economic analogy to call it the wholesale opening-up and enjoyment of nature."[7] He examined the effects of the advancement of transportation on the "psychic life" of the upper strata, both commenting upon and reinforcing the connection between social psychology and social class. In so doing, though, he focused not only upon technology's role in defining humans' changing view of and connection to "nature," but also upon the unethical, life-threatening risks taken by alpinists. He argued that they were mystifying their true motives – exclusion of the masses and a desire for "mere enjoyment" – with an ideological appeal to the educational and moral values ("rugged individualism") of alpine sports.

In another essay, "The Adventure," Simmel discussed adventure as part of our daily existence, but at the same time discussed how, "in its deeper meaning, it occurs outside the usual continuity of this life." He used this dialectic – "the relation between the outer fate and the inner springs of life in which the adventure consists" – to argue that the "fascination of the adventure" was found not in the substance it offered, but rather in "the adventurous form of experiencing it, the intensity and excitement with which it lets us feel life in just this instance." The adventure gets incorporated, not as an accidental happening but as a "normalized" part of everyday life.[8] Comparing the adventurer to the gambler, Simmel showed how in both cases chance and risk can become part of a context of everyday meaning. His move from individualistic social psychology to the more sociological position of explaining what can happen when life as a whole is perceived as an adventure is significant. His interest in the adventure was part of a broader, more all-encompassing interest in leisure and sociability, which, as in Denney's work, makes the strange familiar and the familiar strange.

In "The Sociology of Sociability," the opening speech at the first meeting of the German Sociological Society in October of 1910 in Frankfurt, Simmel emphasized his concern with form and what it symbolizes – the content or message conveyed. Like Denney, Simmel was interested in what play and art could tell us about differently rationalized, and apparently more serious, everyday activities. "Within this constellation, called society, or out of it," Simmel wrote, "there develops a special sociological structure corresponding to those of art and play, which draw their form from these realities but nevertheless leave the reality behind them." Sociability is a key to this line of thinking, not only because it focuses both individual and group needs and how they are brought together, but also because it is "the play form of association and is related to the content-determined concreteness of association as art is related to reality."[9] What are the rights of the individual, the rights of others? What is play, work, art? The answer to these questions rests somewhere in the dynamic emergence of changing boundaries, which are continually being redrawn.

Simmel's interest in association led him to analyze what David Frisby calls "elementary social phenomena."[10] Simmel analyzed mealtimes, letter writing, and even the social significance of the bridge and the door. Both he and Denney were interested in architecture as a medium that permitted and encouraged the transition from one spatial-social setting to another. According to Simmel in his essay "Bridge and Door," the bridge allows us to be aware of the separation of its anchor points while, in correlating separateness and unity, it "always allows the accent to fall on the latter." In contrast, "The door represents in a more decisive manner how separating and connecting are only two sides of precisely the same act."[11] Focusing on the difference of "intention" displayed by the door's opening and closing, and the difference between entering and exiting, Simmel showed how "the door speaks." Denney's work on the architecture of "The Suppliant Skyscrapers" took up similar themes.[12]

It is here – in the attention paid to the connections between different forms and the possibilities they both limit and encourage – that the interests of Denney and Simmel can be joined to the writings of Marshall McLuhan (1911–80). McLuhan, who was born in Edmonton and died in Toronto, was the son of Herbert, a real estate and insurance salesman, and Elsie, an actress and monologist. With Corinne Keller Lewis, whom he married in 1939, he became the father of six children. In the 1930s he did his undergraduate studies at the University of Manitoba, followed by a masters degree at Cambridge University, and he was awarded a Ph.D. from Cambridge in 1942.

McLuhan began his teaching career in the United States at the University of Wisconsin at Madison (1936–37) and St. Louis University in Missouri (1937–44). He returned to Canada in 1944, joining the academic staff of Assumption College, now the University of Windsor, and moved in 1946 to St. Michael's College at the University of Toronto, where, with the exception of 1967–68, when he held an Albert Schweitzer Chair at New York's Fordham University, he spent the remainder of his teaching life. While serving as the founding director of the Centre for Culture and Technology (1963–80) he became a Companion of the Order of Canada (1970), won numerous awards at home and abroad, and became an internationally recognized media guru – to the extent of making a comedic cameo appearance in Woody Allen's film *Annie Hall* (1977).

Although Denney did not attain anything near McLuhan's popularity and fame, he did anticipate several of McLuhan's more interesting ideas. They both spoke about and wrote a good deal on education and the place of technological innovations in schools,[13] and Denney shared McLuhan's intense interest in the new electronic media.

For McLuhan all technology was media, and it all involved extensions of some human faculty. His definition of media was broad enough to encompass everything from the words on the page of this book to the wheel, electronic circuitry, housing, money, clothing, and the dinner fork. McLuhan saw these extensions as constituting environments or technological forms that work to change the everyday lives of human beings. Our perceptions of reality depend upon how information is structured. As Eric McLuhan (his son) and Frank Zingrone put it: "The form of each medium is associated with a different arrangement, or ratio, among the senses, which creates new forms of awareness. These perceptual transformations, the new ways of experiencing that each medium creates, occur in the user regardless of the program content."[14] Thus, as is the case with changes in the function and style of clothing as medium over time and place, the medium becomes both the "message" and the "massage" as it changes us.

These changes are often hidden from consciousness, and McLuhan echoed Denney's idea that time comes from the future with his notion that we march backwards into the future, experiencing the present through "a rear-view mirror." Denney, for his part, appreciated McLuhan's point that media are extensions of human faculties – "wheels" (cars), television as electronic circuitry, and buildings are extensions, respectively, of our feet, central nervous systems, and bodies. This basic insight was often at the bottom of his expressed interest in democracy – specifically, the democratic possibilities of cars, television, and modern architecture.[15]

TV Learning Comes to the Classroom

During the 1950s Denney promoted McLuhan's work, taking a special interest in the new medium of television and its educational possibilities as part of its impact on popular culture. For example, in a paper presented to the Aspen Design Conference Denney praised McLuhan's *The Mechanical Bride* (1951) for approaching popular culture "by way of an historical and humanistic interest in the popular art and rhetoric."[16] McLuhan, Denney said, argued that before anyone could make judgments of particular products, such as the TV commercial, they would have "to define its place in a new universe of perception generated along non-print 'non-linear' principles by the new media." Later Denney elaborated on this line of thought. In a submission to the Federal Communication Corporation Hearings, he again interpreted from McLuhan's *Bride*:

> Mr. McLuhan argues, correctly I think, that critical as well as public sensibility has not caught up with the difference between the way the world appears in print and the way it appears in sound and pictures. The best newspaper in the United States cannot be "put on TV" by any techniques now known, and still make any sense. Vice versa, what TV can do in a few seconds, the best newspaper in the United States could not do in a million words.[17]

Most significantly, perhaps, during the 1950s Denney moved beyond rhetoric and arguments concerning the potential educational value of the new television medium by participating in an innovative experiment that placed television at the centre of the instructional process. In 1955 Stephens College, one of the oldest U.S. institutions of higher learning for women, appointed Denney as its "First Master Teacher" for a course to be taught over closed-circuit TV. Denney spent the fall semester of that year at the Stephens campus in Columbia, Missouri, presenting and refining his thought for "Ideas and Living Together," an interdisciplinary course required for all 850 first-year students. Among the subjects that Denney raised and commented upon were the evaluation of American culture, segregation and integration, swing music, and the summertime phenomenon of men in Bermuda shorts. The goal was in part to provide a more adequate orientation to university life as well as a common intellectual focus for bringing students and faculty together. Another large part of the motivation behind the course was to explore the benefits of bringing the latest in electronic technology to the classroom.

Denney's twenty-minute lectures were picked up by small, versatile television cameras and relayed by cable to fifty classrooms, where other professors with the help of charts, graphs, and other visual aids would spend the last forty minutes of the learning hour leading small discussion groups examining what Denney had said. The experiment was financed by two important grants from the Fund for the Advancement of Education, and, not surprisingly, the Radio Corporation of America (RCA), and the equipment used was to be retained by the College's Radio and Television Department. A report in the *Stephens College News Reporter* (May 1955) outlined the educational philosophy behind the course's TV instruction as elucidated by College president Thomas A. Spragens:

> President Spragens states that he considers television to have unique qualities.... The fact that the television speaker looks every viewer in the eye, and the known capacity of television to eliminate conversation and dominate a social gathering are viewed by President Spragens as potentially great educational assets when properly controlled.
>
> Experiments at Florida State University and a study conducted by Fordham University for the Special Devices Center of the United States Navy have given evidence, he said, that retention from television is greater than that resulting from face-to-face contact with the lecturer. The television technique also improves the possibilities of maximizing the involvement of a large group in a shared intellectual activity, he believes.

Later President Spragens would anticipate today's technology and its digital learning by noting the considerable speculation about the potential of television teaching as a labour-saving device in times of teacher shortages. He also spoke highly of television's ability "to extend," to maximize, "the influence of a superior teacher." By all accounts the Stephens experiment was a success, and in the Denney archives I found several inquiries for information from administrators and faculty at other universities interested in bringing television to the classroom.

Computers and Education at a Distance

McLuhan's "global village" and the "retribalizing" effects of a "cool" medium like television – a medium that requires our participation to get the most out of its potential to inform – have been handed over to the computer. And when we put McLuhan and Simmel together, as Denney did, a realization arises to the effect that technology and sociability influence each other, and consequently they also both influence schooling. A dialectic develops whereby the latest in technology helps to fashion new social contexts, and these contexts create new patterns of sociability that in turn influence educational possibilities. Enter the latest reincarnation of Denney's TV learning: distance education centred in audiovisual and computer-supported instruction.

Today the exciting electronic jolts of the high-tech distance university are not only competing with, but also replacing, what many students see as the slow, too boring, talking-heads tedium of the traditional in-person university.[18] But funnelling resources into education at a distance means reaffirming the so-called "efficiency" of machine technology, replicating computerized thinking in the classroom with the creation of learning "outputs." The problem, as I see it, is that the "learning packages" delivered electronically, from a distance, lead to a kind of pacification of both student and faculty, who become "consumers" inured to the teaching and research dictates of the market.[19]

Both the machine reality and machine mentality created by our use of the computer become central issues here. Taking into account McLuhan's "rear-view mirror," I would argue that creating a "computerized zone," a "microworld" of information "bits" governed by the binary logic basic to computer programming, is a kind of decontextualization that creates a façade of simplicity. The computerized zone is a site in which time and place stand still, and hardly matter, and that leaves little room for ambiguity. For me it is a little like what sharpshooting basketball players describe as "being in a zone." Once in a while, perhaps often depending on the player, they find themselves in a "place" in which, even in an arena packed to the rafters, they don't hear any crowd noise, they feel a supreme sense of confidence, and the basket they are aiming at becomes almost surrealistically huge – so large they can't miss. They find themselves in a kind of "virtual reality" – so much so that as a result, these basketball (and other entertainment) stars who so regularly find themselves "in the zone" sometimes have trouble dealing with the ordinariness of everyday reality. This same principle also explains why heavy computer users sometimes find it difficult to return from their perfect virtual "highs" to the fuzzy ambiguity of real-world relations.[20]

The computer has another effect on education, and especially on learning in schools, one that arises from the ease with which it helps us to generate information. Many observers have pointed out what today is widely known and experienced: we are caught in an information glut – a glut that distracts and confuses us and often just plain overwhelms us.[21]

Most importantly, the computer routinely treats all of this information as being of equal importance. The information seems to emerge from nowhere and everywhere at the same time. This is decontextualization with an emphasis. It makes thinking globally by acting locally extremely difficult, thereby illustrating the McLuhan-Denney awareness that any medium tends to amputate the function that it extends.

In much the same way that television telescopes our view, both extending and narrowing our vision in the same moment, the computer can turn time and place towards the irrelevant. When applied to scholarship, this decontextualization has deleterious effects. For instance, the computer production and manipulation of information can serve to strip away interpretation, reducing the sense of place or location to the computer terminal itself, leading to a sharp loss of meaning. The act of interpretation, the possible subtlety of the information, and the sense of historical moment fall away as both the computer and the zoned or walled microworld that the machine helps to produce deny the most fundamental reality of being human: that knowledge is not only situationally constructed but is also continually changing. Like reason and any other human interaction, the construction of knowledge is a social activity.[22]

Denney's work on the media, learning, and schools anticipated the current emphasis on distance education – an education that with the aid of a computerized technology distances learners by the manner in which it brings them together, making irrelevant their co-presence at the bricks and mortar of a particular institutional place. It would be interesting to have Denney's views on the use of the computer in classrooms today. I would especially like his response to my contention that the sociability of knowledge activity has not only been changed, often for the worse, but also made more difficult by computer-driven education at a distance.

TV, Video Games, and the "Everything Bad Is Good For You" Thesis

In his 2005 book *Everything Bad Is Good For You: How Today's Popular Culture Is Actually Making Us Smarter*, "iconoclastic science writer" Steven Johnson argues that today's computerized and television-dominated life has made us both more interactive and introspective. For me, this idea represents a combination of effects that not only speaks to important changes in patterns of sociability but also undergirds the hype and hope of a technology-centred education at a distance.

Johnson and other like-minded observers of today's popular culture offer a counterargument to some of my views regarding the roles played by both technology and popular culture in our learning.[23] Johnson celebrates the growth of video-gaming, hit television shows, and, most surprisingly, reality TV, arguing that they are all part of a popular culture that is making us smarter. He cites John Dewey's 1938 work on the benefits of collateral learning to argue that the "probing" and "telescoping" required in video-gaming sharpen our intelligence.[24] This argument opposes the contention of some critics that gaming dumbs us down. Johnson elaborates:

> It's not *what* you're thinking about when you're playing a game, it's *the way* you're thinking that matters. ...
>
> Far more than books or movies or music, games force you to make *decisions*. Novels may activate our imagination, and music may conjure up powerful emotions, but games force you to decide, to choose, to prioritize. All the intellectual benefits of gaming derive from this fundamental virtue, because learning how to think is ultimately about learning to

Overtime: Distance Education, Sociability, and the Song of the Sirens • 125 make the right decisions: weighing evidence, analyzing situations, consulting your long-term goals, and then deciding.[25]

With regard to television, and as both Denney and McLuhan were aware, the completion that Johnson sees as necessary in gaming is also found in the "filling in" required of the television audience if it is to experience TV's full potential as an intelligence-inducing medium. Today's television is interactive, just like many of our most popular films. "There's a kind of implicit trust formed between the show and its viewers, a tolerance for planned ambiguity," Johnson says. "That tolerance takes work: you need to be able to make assessments on the fly about the role of each line, putting it in the 'substance' or 'texture' slot. You have to know what you're not supposed to know."[26]

In short, this line of thought goes, recent popular TV shows (*ER, The Sopranos, The Simpsons, Seinfeld*) require more mental labour when compared to their predecessors of times past (*Dragnet, I Love Lucy, The Beverly Hillbillies, Starsky and Hutch, Three's Company*). Furthermore, shows like *The Simpsons* and *Seinfeld* reward the viewer's contemplative intelligence. "The show gets funnier the more you study it," Johnson says, and this is "precisely because the jokes point outside the immediate context of the episode, and because the creators refuse to supply flashing arrows to translate the gags for the uninitiated."[27]

Johnson argues that reality-TV programs feature similar cognitive merits. He urges us to think of these shows in the context of games, and especially the obsession with video games.[28] "Reality television provides the ultimate testimony to the cultural dominance of games in this moment of pop culture history," he writes. He compares video games with the programming of early television, which "took its cues from the stage: three-act dramas, or vaudeville-like acts with rotating skits and musical numbers." Now, "In the Nintendo age, we expect our televised entertainment to take a new form: a series of competitive tests, growing more challenging over time." In the fabulously popular "playoff" programs like *Survivor* and *Fear Factor* and their ilk, as in the gaming, players learn as they play, with rules not being fully established at the outset. As an example he points to *The Apprentice*, a reality TV show that came on the air in winter 2004, hosted by U.S. business (real estate) tycoon-turned-TV-personality Donald Trump. The idea of the program is that Trump conducts a job talent search for a person to head one of his companies: the "ultimate job interview."

> The final round of season one of *The Apprentice*, for instance, threw a monkeywrench into the strategy that had governed the play up until that point, when Trump announced that the two remaining apprentices would have to assemble and manage a team of subordinates who had already been fired in earlier episodes. . . . Suddenly, it wasn't enough just to have clawed your way to the top; you had to have made friends while clawing.[29]

Certainly, an argument can be made that reality TV and the new game shows do tend, somewhat surprisingly, to make mental demands that keep viewers from zoning out in the style of older game shows like *The Price Is Right* and *Wheel of Fortune*. *The Apprentice*, *Survivor*, and similar shows, despite their somewhat shallow premises, require audiences to play along; in so doing they have to keep track of and consequently contribute to the show's social connections. In this sense these shows are both introspective and interactive, or as Johnson puts it: "This is another way in which the reality shows borrow their techniques from the video games: the content is less interesting than the cognitive work the show elicits from your mind. It's the collateral learning that matters."[30]

In addition, the social-network complexity encouraged by today's television, whether it is reality shows or more conventional dramas and comedies, is many times amplified by the presence of the Internet. Viewers wanting to discuss and sort out relationships on *Dallas* or *Three's Company* did not have the luxury of today's followers of *24* or *Lost* as they e-mail, hypertext, instant message, chat-room, or blog their takes on a show's plot evolution and engage, however roughly, with other fans. Still, some of us are less salutary than Johnson about the learning benefits that may accrue from our social networks being broadened in this manner.

I certainly welcome, as I am sure Denney, McLuhan, and Simmel would, an emphasis on sociability as the key to scholarship and learning. I also appreciate that the new technologies offer increased learning opportunities and challenges outside the classroom. But what exactly is the message for educators? Is it that higher education, and perhaps educators at all levels of schooling, should make greater use of the electronic culture? A message along the lines of: use the technology to entertain, and you will educate. I believe that we have to be careful when it comes to our schools getting caught up in passive support of the main technological drift.[31] But if Johnson is correct in arguing that life on the electronic cutting edge is part of a "secular trend" that moves us "toward greater cognitive demands, more depth, more participation,"[32] then questions multiply regarding where all of this leaves school as an institution.

Perhaps too much schooling, like too much partying, may be working the other – the wrong – side of the street. In short, too much schooling may dumb us down. Fan sites devoted to debates and discussions, Net archives where fans compile subtle references found in weekly entertainment shows, special walk-throughs available to those struggling to unravel the puzzles of a new game – all of these are the new "Coles Notes" with an electronic difference. If we agree with Johnson, perhaps we might view all of this as a new kind of scholarship – a view that might make schools, at least in their current form, unnecessary, and schooling increasingly irrelevant. Johnson does not go this far. Rather, he seems to support the idea – one that I would agree with – that potential liberating opportunities are created precisely because schools remain behind today's electronic cutting edge: "The good news, of course, is that kids aren't being exclusively educated by their Nintendo machines or their cell phones. We still have schools and parents to teach wisdom that the popular culture fails to impart."[33]

Popular Culture and Edutainment: The Lonely Crowd Revisited

Popular culture and the cutting-edge technology it embraces are never far from the classroom door. Indeed, most every university in Canada has become a true believer in the pedagogical benefits of applying the latest high-tech innovations. To take but one example, a cover article in a recent edition of the alumni magazine of my alma mater McMaster University, in Hamilton, Ontario, celebrates "Learning without Limits" in a self-congratulatory puff piece featuring the many "tech tools" already in use in their "classroom of the future."[34] A few innovations being employed by McMaster faculty are smart boards, podcasting, wikis, learnlink, and WebCT. The Web Course Tools, "a web-based learning management that allows instructors to deliver their course or components of it on-line," is proudly proclaimed as being in use in "over 600 courses in the faculties of Business, Engineering, Science, Humanities, Health Sciences, Social Science and Continuing Education."

Part of the lure has to do with the speed of technological change and the impact of this change on our learning. Johnson elaborates:

> As the new technologies started to roll out in shorter and shorter cycles, we grew more comfortable with the process of probing a new form of media, learning its idiosyncrasies and its distortions, its symbolic architecture and its rules of engagement. The mind adapts to adaptation. Eventually you get a generation that welcomes the challenge of new technologies, that embraces new genres with a flexibility that would have astonished the semi-panicked audiences that trembled through the first black-and-white films.[35]

What is less often noted, however, is how all this increased flexibility is great for re-energizing capitalist markets and stimulating profitable returns for universities whose business it is to develop consumers, savvy and otherwise. In the Brave New World of celebrated tech change there are, to use a recent popular saying, "no worries," and the "soma" and "feelies" of today's electronic culture make you smarter. They also focus the mind on consuming the latest technological fad as programmed for us. The danger here is that people caught up in this powerful stream will follow, and repeat, the waves of technology-induced behaviour in a less-than-conscious manner that both emulates and is a part of the shorter and shorter cycles of electronic innovation. If we do this, we run the risk of becoming ever more passively programmed in the face of technology-driven and technology-directed programming from afar: in brief, "distance education" and all its drawbacks in spades.

In continuing to think about the similarities and differences of popular culture and school learning, we should note an important perception of difference. The learning experienced through gaming, TV-watching, computer use, and other staples of our popular culture is not forced; it is desired by the participants. After we make the initial choice of what medium to engage with, we may well find that the liberating potential of this voluntary immersion in popular culture, as it is structured by the economics of capital, becomes just as limiting and meagre as the education that results from compulsory attendance at school. And most importantly, this kind of learning comes without many of the traditional school's in-person, non-distancing possibilities for sociability and scholarship.

In this regard the party emphasis of today's higher education is not at all symbolic of a fallen state of being in which we now indulge in cheap pleasures as part of a general degradation of the culture. People are not always drawn to the least complicated entertainment available; and schools, even if they are fast becoming centres of edutainment, just another high-tech consumable of the popular culture industry, are not consciously organized to dumb us down. Still, the observable effects of schooling often make it seem that this is so. "Distance education," education at a distance grounded in the latest technical innovations, is perhaps symptomatic of the direction in which education in general is headed. It seems to me that a comparative study of trends in distance education might be a good place to begin to examine the vision of today's educators and to rethink what we expect from our schools in general, and higher education in particular.[36]

If Johnson and like-minded observers are correct, and most everything we thought bad is good for us, then maybe most of what has been thought good is bad for us. Exhibit "A" might be formal education in schools. And if the broadly based learning once encouraged by a liberal arts education is to be found today in general rules that are learned by probing and exploring the latest in electronic technology, then maybe a technology-centred learning is a remedy for the narrow vocationalism that Denney criticized. Just add technical wizardry to an already highly professionalized university training, mix and *voilà*, we have retooled learners who are the latest reincarnation of Renaissance scholars.

Denney was aware, as I am, that the most recent technological innovation is always resisted for its supposed bad effects. In his day "the bad guy" was television, and in several writings he noted the class and cultural implications of the elite's snobbish concern over television's bad effects on the supposedly less educated and less cultured strata beneath them. In general terms Denney developed a McLuhan-like argument concerning the tension found among readers who believe that "manipulative print outweighs all other kinds" of communication "and that the mass-communication media outweigh the more personal media. To illustrate: it is common for people of some education today to feel that the movies kick print around and that print kicks conversation around – and, one supposes, that talk kicks contemplation around."[37]

In an age in which formal education in schools has become a much required, even much desired consumable, I have to wonder what Denney would make of the contemplation required and encouraged by the new technology that is the focal point of distance education. Does print, as he suggested, remain overprivileged? Can e-mail, the Internet, and videos featuring power point reanimate learners? Can technology at a distance replace "the soul" of in-person instruction at its best? Is that soul lost or merely changed, and to what effect? If, as I have suggested here and argued elsewhere,[38] contemplation is the heart of scholarship, what are the effects upon scholarship of immersion in a screen culture anchored by the computer? Does education at a distance with its accompanying technology make us not only more attuned to popular culture, but also smarter, more intelligent? Does it make us more or less lonely? More or less sociable? More or less other-directed?

Following the publication of *The Lonely Crowd*, several studies were carried out to examine the authors' distinction between the typical character of inner-directed and other-directed individuals.[39] Denney reported: "Studies at Rutgers found that students, if asked about their aspirations, put 'being liked by peers' higher than 'being academically excellent.' While students saw their parents as reversing this order, the parents actually wanted their children to be equally successful in both studies and sociability."[40] The research and other work done since the 1950s have highlighted the continuing importance of sociability as suggested by the work of Denney, Simmel, and McLuhan.[41]

Furthermore, as the schooling of the 1950s and 1960s continues to be replaced by education as entertainment, our closest scrutiny must fall on edutainment, the changing nature of sociability, and the ways in which new technologies alter our learning. Our culture's fascination with the glitz and glamour of the latest technological fix, like its fascination with celebrity, often blinds us. The most important questions tend not to be raised, let alone answered. As someone who has hung around universities and been privileged to interact with students all of my adult life, I am deeply concerned by this condition.

Perhaps, when all is said and done, I am a bit too uptight. I should just learn to relax, to "chill" in modern parlance: join the crowd and the party. Leave behind the troubling questions and scholarly legacy left by thinkers like Denney and those who influenced him and those who came after. Commune in the new high-tech academic grove. If I continue to have trouble participating in e-mail conversations with my students, I could always order a preferred parking sticker and join them in their shopping-mall round of activities, where little distinction is made between shopping at GAP and consuming at the university. With a parking slot guaranteed I could just pop into the university (the campus buildings, that is) every once in a while for a spa-like renewal, complete with some personalized face-to-face classroom interaction. Better yet, I could hit a tailgate party before and after – and maybe even in the middle of – the Big Homecoming Game. Bratwurst and beer: sounds good to me.

But maybe that's just a little too tongue-in-cheek. I don't really want to party my way out of the lonely crowd and into acceptance and conformity – even though being a part of the main drift is hard to avoid. The way in which today's dominant institutions interlock to form a fun culture, dominated by entertainment and party lifestyles, makes resistance on a personal level difficult. But we can talk to each other and at least begin to take action collectively to remedy the most damaging aspects of today's higher education. Better yet, let us together make a concerted effort to resist edutainment and classroom commercialization in favour of university autonomy and a return to the sociability of serious scholarship – which is, by definition, critical. Let's engage in a learning and teaching that works in opposition to an academic lifestyle created and dominated by (or created from the cloth of) popular culture. A higher education environment re-energized and driven by scholarship will not only benefit the university as an educational institution but also, and most importantly, better serve the needs of the public at large.

Notes

1 "The Party's the Thing"

1. Heath and Potter, *Rebel Sell*, p.9.
2. Alix Kates Shulman, "Dances with Feminists," *Women's Review of Books* 9:3 (December 1991), explains how the quotation "If I can't dance I don't want to be in your revolution" came to be attributed to Emma Goldman. See: <http://sunsite.berkeley.edu/Goldman/Features/dances_shulman.html>. Though, Shulman says, the sentiment was clearly Emma Goldman's, she did not write this statement or any of its variations. The response of Goldman to "the boy" appears in her biography, *Living My Life* (1931), p.56.
3. Goldman, *Living My Life*, p.56.
4. *The New Shorter Oxford English Dictionary*, p.3205.
5. Judd, "College Football – Tailgating – Prefer Pork or Pâté?" p.F17.
6. Frederick, Jr., "A Good Day To Be Here: Tailgating in The Grove at Ole Miss," pp.73–74.
7. See Gans, "Best-Sellers by Sociologists."
8. Balsley, "Hot-Rod Culture"; Denny, *Astonished Muse*, pp.138–56.
9. Denney, *Astonished Muse*, p.138.
10. Ibid., pp.153, 154.
11. Denney, "Leisure Society," p.46.
12. Denney, *Astonished Muse*, pp.25–26.
13. Denney, *Astonished Muse*, p.99.
14. Denney, "American Youth Today," p.126.
15. Twitchell, *Branded Nation*, p.125.
16. See Shiva, *Monocultures of the Mind,* and Ritzer, *The McDonaldization of Society*, for earlier important work on the homogenization theme.
17. Denney, "The American Consumer – Slave or Rebel?" transcript, p.2.
18. For small-town coverage, see *Chronicle-Journal* (Thunder Bay, Ont.), Nov. 18, 2006, pp.D1, D7; *Peterborough Examiner*, Nov. 17, 2006, pp.A1, A5.

2 Cultural Studies

1. Lynes's book did not have a subtitle in the 1949 edition; but a later, 1989, edition had as its complete title: *The Tastemakers: The Shaping of American Popular Taste.*
2. Denney quoted in Quagliano, *Feast of Strangers*, pp.11–12. Page numbers referred to here and below are from Denney in Quagliano unless otherwise noted.
3. Ibid., p.4.

4   Ibid., p.1.
5   Ibid., p.12.
6   Ibid., p. 9.
7   Ibid., pp.35–36.
8   Ibid., p.13.
9   Ibid.
10 Ibid., p.18.
11 Ibid., p.20.
12 Ibid., pp.22–23.
13 Ibid., p.19.
14 Ibid., pp.19, 40.
15 Ibid., p. 41.
16 Ibid., pp.24, 42.
17 Ibid., p.42.
18 Ibid., p.45.
19 Ibid., p.46. Father Coughlin (1891–1979) was pastor at the Shrine of the Little Flower in Royal Oak, Michigan, from 1926 to 1966. He was a Hamilton, Ontario–born Roman Catholic priest who beginning in 1926 broadcast a weekly radio program in the United States that drew millions of listeners during the 1930s. He became increasingly political and by 1942 he was ordered by the church hierarchy to cease all non-religious activities. An increasing anti-Semitism and fanaticism fuelled his political views. He blamed Jewish financiers for the U.S. entry into World War II, and his criticism of the New Deal and FDR's other policies was, according to my source, both vehement and unrelenting.
20 Denney, *Astonished Muse*, p.3.
21 See Lynes, *Tastemakers*.
22 See Denney, *Astonished Muse*, pp.204–23.
23 Ibid., p.99.
24 Ibid.
25 Ibid., p.153.
26 Ibid., p.26.
27 Ibid., p.207.
28 Ibid., pp.215, 222.
29 Ibid., p.111.
30 Riesman and Denney, "Football in America," p.318.
31 Denney, *Astonished Muse*, p.145.
32 Ibid., p.142.
33 See Nelsen, *Schooling as Entertainment*, pp.44–50.
34 McLuhan, "Speed of Cultural Change," p.18.
35 See "A Marshall McLuhan Reading List" in McLuhan and Zingrone, eds., *Essential McLuhan*, pp.397–401.
36 McLuhan, *Understanding Media*, p.164.
37 Denney, *Astonished Muse*, p.235.
38 Ibid., p.237.
39 See, for instance, Gitlin, *Whole World Is Watching*.
40 See Owram, *Born at the Right Time*; and Kostash, *Long Way from Home*.
41 Elsewhere, in beginning to make a case for a Denney postmodern, I have

expanded my review of his prose by examining some of his poetry (especially Denney, *In Praise of Adam: Poems by Reuel Denney*): see Nelsen, *Schooling as Entertainment*, pp.40, 51–53.
42 For Bourdieu, see "Cultural Reproduction and Social Reproduction."
43 Denney in Quagliano, *Feast of Strangers*, p.34.
44 Evory, "Reuel Denney," p.166.
45 Denney in Quagliano, *Feast of Strangers*, p.96.

3 The Party Hits the Road

1 Seiler, "Anxiety and Automobility," pp.27–28.
2 Daniel I. Vieyra's work on architectural changes in America's roadside lodging provides a good illustration of this impact. See Vieyra, "Architecture of America's Roadside Lodging."
3 Vieyra, "Architecture of America's Roadside Lodging," pp.15, 16.
4 Wilson, *Culture of Nature*, p.91.
5 Swift, "Rush to Nowhere," p.10.
6 Jackson, *Crabgrass Frontier*, p.176.
7 Vieyra, "Architecture of America's Roadside Lodging," p.21.
8 Lower, *Canadians in the Making*, p.425.
9 Vieyra, "Architecture of America's Roadside Lodging," p.37.
10 Boorstin, *Image or What Happened to the American Dream*.
11 Vieyra, "Architecture of America's Roadside Lodging," pp.60, 123.
12 Statistics Canada, *Historical Statistics of Canada*, Series T147–94.
13 Seiler, Anxiety and Automobility," p.110.
14 Ibid., pp.88–108.
15 As discussed in Seiler, "Anxiety and Automobility," pp.211–48.
16 Marcuse, *One-Dimensional Man*.
17 Foucault, *Discipline and Punish*.
18 Niedzviecki, *Hello, I'm Special*.
19 Seiler, *Anxiety and Automobility*, pp.231, 233.
20 In the mid-twentieth century the annual publication *Travelguide*, offering advice for black motorists, had the motto "Vacation and Recreation without Humiliation."
21 Gilroy, "Driving While Black," p.84.
22 Ibid., p.90.
23 Ibid., p.94.
24 Ibid., pp.94, 98.
25 Ibid., p.100.
26 Seiler, "Anxiety and Automobility," p.105.
27 Twitchell, *Branded Nation*, p.125.
28 See, for instance, Wolff, "On the Road Again: Metaphors of Travel in Cultural Criticism"; Frederick and MacLeod, *Women and the Journey*; Gordon, *Good Boys and Dead Girls and Other Essays*; May, *Homeward Bound: American Families in the Cold War Era*; and Kolodny, *The Lay of the Land: Metaphors of Experience and History in American Life and Letters*.
29 Balsley, "Hot-Rod Culture," pp.353–55.

30 Ibid., p.357.
31 Denney, *Astonished Muse*, p.153.
32 Wolfe, *Kandy-Kolored Tangerine-Flake Streamline Baby*, p.90.
33 Denney, *Astonished Muse*, pp.148–49.
34 Wolfe, *Kandy-Kolored Tangerine-Flake Streamline Baby*, pp.101, 98.
35 Denney, *Astonished Muse*, p.153.
36 Ibid., p.152.
37 Schmidt, *Disciplined Minds*.

4 Big Games

1 For partial data, see *The Globe and Mail*, Dec. 28, 2005, p.S4.
2 Denney, *Astonished Muse*, p.103.
3 Oriard, *Reading Football*, p.23.
4 Cochem, "Something New in Football," p.88.
5 See Oriard, *Reading Football*, pp.35–37.
6 Ibid., pp.44, 43.
7 Ibid; emphasis in original.
8 See Taylor, *Principles of Scientific Management*.
9 The flying wedge formation allowed teammates to link together in what has been described as "a high-speed play of mass momentum." Many players wore a specialized flying wedge belt equipped with handles. The play was first run by Harvard against Yale in their annual game in 1892. On quarterback Bernie Trafford's signal, two groups raced forward and converged, forming a V in front of Trafford, who handed the ball off to his fullback, Charlie Brewer. The entire Harvard team then moved forward as one, with ball carrier Brewer shielded by the protective wall of teammates' bodies. Harvard gained thirty yards. The play was designed by Loren Deland, a Harvard graduate and Boston businessman, to counter the spirited ferocity and athleticism of Yale's great defensive stopper, Frank Hinkey. By the start of the 1894 season the flying wedge as well as the special belts with handles had been outlawed by the national rules committee.
10 Denney, *Astonished Muse*, p.114.
11 DeLillo, *End Zone*, pp.35–36, 132–33.
12 Shaw, *Meat on the Hoof*.
13 Oriard, *Reading Football*, pp.61–62.
14 Ibid.
15 Ibid., p.101; emphasis added.
16 Ibid., p.129; Oriard includes a short 183-word *Oregonian* story in its entirety.
17 Denney, *Astonished Muse*, pp.104, 105.
18 Ibid., p.120.
19 Denney, "Feast of Strangers," p.251.

5 Tailgating

1. For example, Wrong, "Oversocialized Conception of Man in Sociology."
2. Frederick, "Good Day to Be Here," pp.50–51.
3. The description of the Grove is from the university's website: <http://www.olemiss.edu/gameday/grovesociety>; the quotation "wanted his players to share . . . " is from Frederick, "Good Day to Be Here."
4. Frederick, "Good Day to Be Here."
5. Ibid., pp.18, 53–55; emphasis added.
6. Bellah, *Habits of the Heart*; Putnam, *Bowling Alone*.
7. Frederick, "Good Day to Be Here," p.61.
8. Mills, *Power Elite*; Bradsher, *High and Mighty*. Bradsher documents the marketing story of how the SUV industry has been able to escape regulation and continue feverish production of its unsafe death-producing machines.
9. Heath and Potter, *Rebel Sells*; Niedzviecki, *Hello, I'm Special*.
10. *The Toronto Sun*, Feb. 15, 2004, p.T9.
11. Gale Group, "Tailgating Encouraged for Almost Any Occasion."
12. Quoted in Chow, "Asphalt Fare," *National Post* (Toronto), Jan. 17, 2005, pp.FP1, 11.
13. Ibid.
14. Galpin Motors website: <http://www.galpin.com>.
15. Chow, "Asphalt Fare."
16. "Tailgating: Hold the $1,000 Donation," *Register-Guard* (Eugene, Ore.), Oct. 15, 2004.
17. Noted by Judd, "College Football – Tailgating – Prefer Pork or Pâté?"
18. Frederick, "Good Day to Be Here," pp.72, 73.
19. Profiled by Rebecca Nolan, "Tailgating Pro Tackles Eugene," *Register-Guard*, Oct. 17, 2004.
20. Denney, *Astonished Muse*, pp.104, 120.
21. Ibid., pp.112,113.
22. Ibid., p.117.
23. Frederick, "Good Day to Be Here."
24. See p.54 here.
25. Judd, "College Football – Tailgating – Prefer Pork or Pâté?" p.F17.
26. Frederick, "Good Day to Be Here," pp.68, 66.
27. Ibid., p.57.
28. Ibid.

6 The Fourth Quarter

1. Oldenburg, *Great Good Place*, p.xxix.
2. Ibid., pp.10, 13.
3. Riesman and Denney, "Football in America," pp.318, 317.
4. Ibid., p. 317.
5. Sperber, *Beer and Circus*, pp.56–57.
6. Ibid., p.58.
7. Ibid.

8 Ibid., p.59.
9 See Dreyer, "Group Asks for End to 'Party School' Lists."
10 Slater, "More Work on Fridays? GIVE ME A BREAK," *Oregon Daily Emerald*, Nov. 7, 2005; Slater's article, an opinion piece in a student newspaper, was reporting on a *New York Times* story.
11 Penn State, "Student Drinking."
12 "Semester Abroad Spent Drinking with Other American Students," *The Onion*, Feb. 13, 2002.
13 Denney, "American Youth Today," p.127.
14 Bruneau, "University Ratings Distort Higher Education," p.A11; see also Bruneau and Savage, *Counting Out the Scholars*.
15 Twitchell, *Branded Nation*, p.165.
16 Nelsen, *Miseducating*, pp.41–63; Nelsen, *Schooling as Entertainment*, pp.121–42.
17 I further develop these ideas in Nelsen, *Schooling as Entertainment*, p.122.
18 Denney, "American Youth Today," pp.126, 124; see also p.13 here.
19 Denney, "American Youth Today."
20 Powell, Farrar, and Cohen, *Shopping Mall High School*, p.12.
21 Twitchell, *Branded Nation*, p.169.
22 See, for instance, "The Yale Report of 1828: Part I, Liberal Education and Collegiate Life," in the Collegiate Way website: <http://collegiateway.org/reading/yale-report-1828/>.
23 Gatto, *Dumbing Us Down*.
24 Denney, "American Youth Today," pp.128–29. This theme was later taken up by E.D. Hirsch, Jr., *Cultural Literacy* (1987), but, I believe, not in the same way in which Denney might have elaborated on it.
25 Denney, "Learner and His Audience," p.29.
26 Denney, "American Youth Today," pp.137, 131.
27 Schmidt, *Disciplined Minds*. Elsewhere, I have offered my own critique of professionalism; see Nelsen, *Miseducating*, pp.151–73, 204–37; Nelsen, "Community College Con," pp.336–57.
28 Noble, *Digital Diploma Mills*, p.2.
29 Denney, "American Youth Today," p.128.
30 Ibid., p.140.
31 Freeman, *Over-Educated American*; Schwartz, *Overskill*; Livingstone, *Education-Jobs Gap*.
32 See, for instance, my earlier work in Nelsen, "Books, Boredom, and Behind Bars."
33 Denney, "American Youth Today," p.141.
34 Sperber, *Beer and Circus*, p.56.
35 William S. Saum, "Sports Gambling in College." Saum was Director of Agent, Gambling and Amateurism Activities for the National Collegiate Athletic Association. The research at Harvard University was done by Howard Shaffer.
36 See, for example, Barnes et al., "Effects of Alcohol Misuse on Gambling Patterns in Youth." On student gambling, see also Isenberg, "Gambling on College Sports"; Layden, "Campus Gambling – Better Education"; Sperber, *Beer and Circus*; and Saum, "Sports Gambling in College."

37 See StudentDrinkingGames.com.
38 Theocshow.com.
39 Johnson, *Everything Bad Is Good for You*.
40 Suellentrop, "Madden: Sports' New Arbiter of Cool."
41 Gillette, "All I Really Need to Know about Football."
42 See Suellentrop, "Madden: Sports' New Arbiter of Cool."
43 Denney, "American Youth Today," p.128.
44 See Franks, *Conquest of Cool*.

7 Overtime

1 Denney, "Beyond the Learning and the Doing: Notes on Dialogue between Age and Youth Today," p.3.
2 Denney, *Astonished Muse*, p.4.
3 Denney, "Beyond the Learning and the Doing," p.6.
4 Ibid., p.11.
5 Knutilla, *Sociology Revisited*, p.130.
6 Frisby, *Georg Simmel*, p.14.
7 Simmel in Frisby and Featherstone, eds., *Simmel on Culture*, p.219.
8 Simmel in ibid., pp.222, 229, 230.
9 Simmel in ibid., p.120.
10 Frisby, *Simmel and Since*, p.41.
11 In Frisby and Featherstone, eds., *Simmel on Culture*, p.172.
12 Denney, *Astonished Muse*, pp.224–41.
13 See McLuhan's bibliography in Eric McLuhan and Zingrone, eds., *Essential McLuhan*.
14 Eric McLuhan and Zingrone, eds., *Essential McLuhan*, p.3.
15 See chapters 7, 8, 11 in Denney, *Astonished Muse*.
16 Denney, "Development of an Inquiry," p.14.
17 Denney, "Statement of Reuel Denney in FCC Hearings," p.13, footnote 3.
18 See, for instance, Nelsen, "Reading, Writing and Relationships among the Electronic Zealots," pp.184–210, in which I critique this "education at a distance," offering stories from my workplace.
19 Nelsen, "Reading, Writing and Relationships among the Electronic Zealots," p.187.
20 Ibid., p.196.
21 See, for example, Roszak, *Cult of Information*, for early thinking on the effects of the cult of information.
22 Nelsen, "Reading, Writing and Relationships among the Electronic Zealots," pp.196–97.
23 Johnson, *Everything Bad Is Good for You*. For others in this same vein, see Gee, *What Video Games Have to Teach Us about Learning and Literacy*; Spencer, *Two Aspirins and a Comedy*.
24 Dewey, *Experience and Education*.
25 Johnson, *Everything Bad Is Good for You*, pp.40–41.
26 Ibid., pp.81–82.
27 Ibid., p.87.

28 Ibid., pp.92–93.
29 Ibid., p.93.
30 Ibid., p.107.
31 Nelsen, *Miseducating*; Nelsen, *Schooling as Entertainment*.
32 Johnson, *Everything Bad Is Good for You*, p.157.
33 Ibid., pp.187–88.
34 See Bowness, "Learning without Limits," pp.11–14.
35 Johnson, *Everything Bad Is Good for You*, p.178.
36 See Noble, *Digital Diploma Mills*.
37 Denney, "Cultural Context of Print in the Communications Revolution," p.378.
38 Nelsen, "Marking Time in Computopia"; Nelsen, "Reading, Writing and Relationships among the Electronic Zealots."
39 Riley, Riley, and Moore, "Adolescent Values and the Riesman Typology"; Sofer, "Inner-Direction, Other-Direction and Autonomy"; Coleman, *Adolescent Society*; Johnstone, *Popular Music and the Adolescent*.
40 Denney, "Beyond the Learning and the Doing," p.32.
41 For examples of other work, see Bellah et al., *Habits of the Heart*; Oldenburg, *Great Good Place*; Putnam, *Bowling Alone*.

Bibliography

Arendt, Hannah. *The Human Condition*. Chicago: University of Chicago Press, 1958.

Balsley, Gene. "The Hot-Rod Culture." *American Quarterly* 2 (1950): 353–58.

Barnes, G.M. et al. "Effects of Alcohol Misuse on Gambling Patterns in Youth." *Journal of Studies on Alcohol* 63 (2002): 767–75.

Bellah, Robert N. et al. *Habits of the Heart: Individualism and Commitment in American Life*. New York: Harper & Row, 1985.

Boorstin, Daniel J. *The Image or What Happened to the American Dream*. New York: Atheneum, 1962.

Bourdieu, Pierre. "Cultural Reproduction and Social Reproduction." In *Power and Ideology in Education*, ed. Jerome Karabel and A.H. Halsey. New York: Oxford University Press, 1977.

Bowness, Sue. "Learning Without Limits." *McMaster Times: The Newsmagazine for McMaster University Alumni*, Spring 2006.

Bradsher, Keith. *High and Mighty: The Dangerous Rise of the SUV*. New York: Public Affairs (Perseus Books), 2002.

Bruneau, William. "University Ratings Distort Higher Education." *CAUT Bulletin*, January 2006.

———— and Donald C. Savage. *Counting Out the Scholars: The Case against Performance Indicators in Higher Education*. Toronto: James Lorimer, 2002.

Chow, Jason. "Asphalt Fare: Football Tailgating Goes Upscale." *National Post* (Toronto), Jan. 17, 2005.

Cochem, E.M. "Something New in Football." *Outing* 61 (1912): 88–92.

Coleman, James S. *The Adolescent Society: The Social Life of the Teenager and Its Impact on Education*. Glencoe, Ill.: The Free Press, 1961.

DeLillo, Don. *End Zone*. New York: Houghton Mifflin, 1972.

Denney, Reuel. *The Connecticut River and Other Poems*. New Haven, Conn.: Yale University Press, 1939.

————. *The Astonished Muse*. Chicago: University of Chicago Press, 1964 [1957].

————. "The Development of an Inquiry: Locating and Defining the Problems of Modern Mass Communications." Paper delivered at Conference on Popular Culture and the Mass Media – Aspen Design Conference. Aspen, Col., 1954.

————. "The Cultural Context of Print in the Communications Revolution." *The Library Quarterly* 25 (1955): 376–83.

————. "The American Consumer – Slave or Rebel?" Radio Transcript. London: BBC, Aug. 14, 1958.

———. "The Leisure Society." *Harvard Business Review* 37 (1959): 46–60.

———. "Statement of Reuel Denney in FCC Hearings." Washington, D.C.: Federal Communications Commission, Dec. 11, 1959.

———. *In Praise of Adam: Poems by Reuel Denney*. Chicago: University of Chicago Press, 1961.

———. "American Youth Today: A Bigger Cast, a Wider Screen." *Daedalus* (Special Issue, "Youth: Change and Challenge," ed. Stephen R. Graubard) 91,1 (Winter 1962): 124–44.

———. "Beyond the Learning and the Doing: Notes on Dialogue between Age and Youth Today." Paper delivered at Conference on the Nuclear-Scientific Era: The Child and Education, New York, Auspices Walden School, April 25, 1964.

———. "The Learner and His Audience." *Social Forces*, 1964: 24–34.

———. "Feast of Strangers: Varieties of Social Experience in America." In *On the Making of Americans: Essays in Honor of David Riesman*, ed. Herbert J. Gans et al. Philadelphia: University of Pennsylvania Press, 1979.

———. "Experience in the World." In *Feast of Strangers: Selected Prose and Poetry of Reuel Denney*, ed. Tony Quagliano. Westport, Conn.: Greenwood Press, 1999.

Dewey, John. *Experience and Education*. New York: Simon & Schuster (Touchstone), 1997 [1938].

Dreyer, Nicole. "Group Asks for End to 'Party School' Lists." *Daily Texan* (Austin), Aug. 14, 2002.

Evory, Ann. "Reuel Denney." *Contemporary Authors* 2 (1981): 165–66.

Foucault, Michel. *Discipline and Punish: The Birth of the Prison*. Trans. Alan Seridan. New York: Pantheon Books, 1978.

Franks, Thomas. *The Conquest of Cool: Business Culture, Counterculture and the Rise of Hip Consumerism*. Chicago: University of Chicago Press, 1997.

Frederick, Bonnie and Susan H. Macleod, eds. *Women and the Journey*. Pullman: Washington State University Press, 1993.

Frederick, Charles R., Jr. "A Good Day to Be Here: Tailgating in the Grove at Ole Miss." Unpublished Ph.D. dissertation, Indiana University, Bloomington, 1999.

Freeman, Richard B. *The Over-Educated American*. New York: Academic Press, 1976.

Frisby, David. *Georg Simmel*. London: Tavistock, 1984.

———. *Simmel and Since: Essays on Georg Simmel's Social Theory*. London: Routledge, 1992.

——— and Mike Featherstone, eds. *Simmel on Culture: Selected Writings*. London: Sage, 1997.

Gale Group. "Tailgating Encouraged for Almost Any Occasion: The Grill Industry Fans the Flames, Even Without a Game To Watch." Article by Thyra Porter. Fairchild Publications, Aug. 23, 2004.

Gans, Herbert J. "Best-Sellers by Sociologists: An Exploratory Study." *Contemporary Sociology* 26 (1997): 131–35.

Gatto, John Taylor. *Dumbing Us Down: The Hidden Curriculum of Compulsory Schooling*. Philadelphia: New Society Publishers, 1992.

Gee, James Paul. *What Video Games Have to Teach Us about Learning and Literacy*. New York: Palgrave, 2003.

Gillette, Felix. "All I Really Need To Know About Football." <http://www.slate.com/id/2148548/> 2006.

Gilroy, Paul. "Driving While Black." In *Car Cultures*, ed. Daniel Miller. New York: Oxford University Press, 2001.

Gitlin, Todd. *The Whole World Is Watching: Mass Media in the Making and Unmaking of the New Left*. Berkeley: University of California Press, 1980.

Globe and Mail, The. Dec. 28, 2005: S4.

Goldman, Emma. *Living My Life*. New York: Alfred Knopf, 1931.

Goodman, Paul. *Growing Up Absurd: Problems of Youth in the Organized System*. New York: Random House, 1960.

Gordon, Mary. *Good Boys and Dead Girls and Other Essays*. New York: Viking, 1991.

Handlin, Oscar. *The Uprooted: The Epic Story of the Great Migrations That Made the American People*. New York: Grosset & Dunlap, 1951.

Heath, Joseph and Andrew Potter. *The Rebel Sell: Why the Culture Can't Be Jammed*. Toronto: Harper Collins, 2004.

Hirsch, E.D., Jr. *Cultural Literacy: What Every American Needs to Know*. New York: Houghton Mifflin Company, 1987.

Hoffer, Eric. *The True Believer: Thoughts on the Nature of Mass Movements*. New York: Harper, 1951.

Hollingshead, August B. *Elmtown's Youth: The Impact of Social Classes on Adolescents*. New York: John Wiley & Sons, 1949.

Hsu, Francis L.K. *Clan, Caste, and Club: A Comparative Study of Chinese, Hindu, and American Ways of Life*. Toronto: D. Van Nostrand Company (Canada), 1963.

Isenberg, Marc. "Gambling on College Sports: The NCAA's Solution Is Part of the Problem." <http://nabc.cstv.com/nabcprograms-gambling-awareness.html>, 2006.

Jackson, Kenneth T. *Crabgrass Frontier: The Suburbanization of the United States*. New York: Oxford University Press, 1985.

Johnson, Steven. *Everything Bad Is Good For You: How Today's Popular Culture Is Actually Making Us Smarter*. New York: Riverhead Books (Penguin), 2005.

Johnstone, John. *Popular Music and the Adolescent*. Chicago: University of Chicago, Committee on Communication, 1955.

Judd, Ron C. "College Football – Tailgating – Prefer Pork or Pâté? UW Fan Fare Reveals Their Lot in Life." *Seattle Times*, Aug. 28, 1996.

Kerouac, Jack. *On the Road*. New York: Viking Press, 1957.

Knutilla, Murray. *Sociology Revisited: Basic Concepts and Perspectives*. Toronto: McClelland and Stewart, 1993.

Kolodny, Annette. *The Lay of the Land: Metaphors of Experience and History in American Life and Letters*. Chapel Hill: University of North Carolina Press, 1975.

Kostash, Myrna. *Long Way from Home: The Story of the Sixties Generation in Canada*. Toronto: James Lorimer and Company, 1980.

Layden, Tim. "Campus Gambling – Better Education – First of Three Parts." *Sports Illustrated*, April 3, 1995.

Lévi-Strauss, Claude. *Structural Anthropology*. Trans. Claire Jacobson and Brooke Grundfest Schoepf. Garden City, N.Y.: Doubleday & Company, 1963.

Livingstone, D.W. *The Education-Jobs Gap: Underemployment or Economic Democracy*. Toronto: Garamond, 1999.

Lynes, Russell. *The Tastemakers*. New York: Harper & Brothers, 1949.

Marcuse, Herbert. *One-Dimensional Man: Studies in the Ideology of Advanced Industrial Society*. Boston: Beacon Press, 1964.

Matson, Floyd W. *The Broken Image: Man, Science and Society*. New York: George Braziller, 1964.

May, Elaine Tyler. *Homeward Bound: American Families in the Cold War Era*. New York: Basic Books, 1988.

McLuhan, Eric and Frank Zingrone, eds. *The Essential McLuhan*. New York: Basic Books, 1995.

McLuhan, Marshall. *The Mechanical Bride*. New York: Vanguard Press, 1951.

———. "Speed of Cultural Change." *College Composition and Communication* 9 (1958):16–20.

———. *Understanding Media: The Extensions of Man*. Toronto: McGraw-Hill, 1964.

Mills, C. Wright. *The Power Elite*. New York: Oxford, 1956.

Nelsen, Randle W. "Books, Boredom, and Behind Bars: An Explanation of Apathy and Hostility in Our Schools." *Canadian Journal of Education/Revue Canadienne de l'Education* 10:2 (1985).

———. "Marking Time in Computopia: The Edubusiness University Revisited." *Society/Société* 14:3 (1990).

———. *Miseducating: Death of the Sensible*. Kingston, Ont.: Cedarcreek Publications, 1991.

———. "Reading, Writing and Relationships among the Electronic Zealots: Distance Education and the Traditional University." In *Inside Canadian Universities: Another Day at the Plant*, ed. Randle W. Nelsen. Kingston, Ont.: Cedarcreek Publications 1997.

———. *Schooling as Entertainment: Corporate Education Meets Popular Culture*. Kingston, Ont.: Cedarcreek Publications, 2002.

———. "The Community College Con: 'Education That Works'?" In *The Professionalization of Work*, ed. Merle Jacobs and Stephen E. Bosanac. Whitby, Ont.: de Sitter Publications, 2006.

New Shorter Oxford English Dictionary. Ed. Lesley Brown. Oxford: Clarendon Press, 1993.

Nicolson, Harold. *Good Behaviour*. Boston: Beacon Press, 1960 [1955].

Niedzviecki, Hal. *Hello, I'm Special: How Individuality Became the New Conformity*. Toronto: Penguin, 2004.

Noble, David F. *Digital Diploma Mills: The Automation of Higher Education.* Toronto: Between the Lines, 2002.
Nolan, Rebecca. "Tailgating Pro Tackles Eugene." *Register-Guard* (Eugene, Ore.), Oct. 17, 2004.
Oldenburg, Ray. *The Great Good Place.* New York: Marlowe & Company, 1997.
Onion, The. "Semester Abroad Spent Drinking with Other American Students," Feb. 13, 2002.
Oriard, Michael. *Reading Football: How the Popular Press Created an American Spectacle.* Chapel Hill: University of North Carolina Press, 1993.
Owram, Doug. *Born at the Right Time: A History of the Baby-Boom Generation.* Toronto: University of Toronto Press, 1996.
Penn State, Division of Student Affairs. "Student Drinking." *Penn State Pulse,* February 2004.
Pitt-Rivers, J.A. *The People of the Sierra.* Chicago: University of Chicago Press, 1961.
Postman, Neil. *The Disappearance of Childhood.* New York: Delacorte, 1982.
Powell, Arthur G., Eleanor Farrar, and David K. Cohen. *The Shopping Mall High School: Winners and Losers in the Educational Marketplace.* Boston: Houghton Mifflin, 1985.
Putnam, Robert D. *Bowling Alone: The Collapse and Revival of American Community.* New York: Simon & Schuster, 2000.
Quagliano, Tony. *Feast of Strangers: Selected Prose and Poetry of Reuel Denney.* Westport, Conn.: Greenwood Press, 1999.
Register-Guard, The (Eugene, Ore.). "Tailgating, Hold the $1,000 Donation," Oct. 15, 2004.
Riesman, David and Reuel Denney. "Football in America: A Study in Culture Diffusion." *American Quarterly* 3 (1951): 309–25.
———. Reuel Denney, and Nathan Glazer. *The Lonely Crowd: A Study of the Changing American Character.* New Haven, Conn.: Yale University Press, 1950.
Riley, Matilda White, John W. Riley, and Mary E. Moore. "Adolescent Values and the Riesman Typology." In *Culture and Social Character: The Work of David Riesman,* ed. Seymour Martin Lipset and Leo Lowenthal. Glencoe, Ill.: The Free Press, 1961.
Ritzer, George. *The McDonaldization of Society: An Investigation into the Changing Character of Contemporary Social Life.* Thousand Oaks, Cal.: Pine Forge, 1993.
Roszak, Theodore. *The Cult of Information: The Folklore of Computers and the True Art of Thinking.* New York: Pantheon, 1986.
Saum, William S. "Sports Gambling in College: Cracking Down on Illegal Betting." <http://www.findarticles.com/p/articles/mi_m1272/is_2650_128/ai_55149352>, 1999.
Schmidt, Jeff. *Disciplined Minds: A Critical Look at Salaried Professionals and the Soul-Battering System That Shapes Their Lives.* Lanham, Md.: Rowman and Littlefield, 2000.

Schwartz, Eugene S. *Overskill: The Decline of Technology in Modern Civilization*. Chicago: Quadrangle Books, 1971.

Seiler, Cotton. "Anxiety and Automobility: Cold War Individualism and the Interstate Highway System." Unpublished Ph.D. dissertation, University of Kansas, Lawrence, 2002.

Shaw, Gary. *Meat on the Hoof: The Hidden World of Texas Football*. New York: Dell, 1972.

Shiva, Vandana. *Monocultures of the Mind: Perspectives on Biodiversity and Biotechnology*. London: Zed Books, 1993.

Slater, Alice. "More Work on Fridays? Give Me a Break." *Oregon Daily Emerald* (Eugene, Ore.), Nov. 7, 2005.

Sofer, Elaine Graham. "Inner-Direction, Other-Direction and Autonomy: A Study of College Students." In *Culture and Social Character: The Work of David Riesman*, ed. Seymour Martin Lipset and Leo Lowenthal. Glencoe, Ill.: The Free Press, 1961.

Spencer, Metta. *Two Aspirins and a Comedy: How Television Can Enhance Health and Society*. Boulder, Col.: Paradigm, 2006.

Sperber, Murray. *Beer and Circus: How Big-Time College Sports Is Crippling Undergraduate Education*. New York: Henry Holt and Company, 2000.

Statistics Canada, *Historical Statistics of Canada*. Series T147–94.

Stephens College News Reporter (Columbia, Miss.) 14,4 (May 1955).

StudentDrinkingGames.com website.

Suellentrop, Chris. "Madden: Sports' New Arbiter of Cool." Internet posting, Aug. 14, 2003.

Swift, Richard. "Rush to Nowhere." *New Internationalist* 343 (March 2002).

Taylor, Frederick Winslow. *The Principles of Scientific Management*. New York: Harper & Brothers, 1911.

Tocqueville, Alexis de. *Democracy in America*. Vols. 1, 2. New York: Vintage Books, 1960 [1835, 1840].

Toronto Sun, Feb. 15, 2004, p.T9.

Travelguide. "Vacation and Recreation without Humiliation." Annual guidebook, 1947–57.

Twitchell, James B. *Branded Nation: The Marketing of Megachurch, College Inc., and Museumworld*. New York: Simon & Schuster, 2004.

Veblen, Thorstein. *The Theory of the Leisure Class*. London: Dover Publications, 1994 [1899].

———. *The Theory of Business Enterprise*. New York: Charles Scribner's Sons, 1904.

———. *The Higher Learning in America: A Memorandum on the Conduct of Universities by Business Men*. New York: Hill and Wang, 1957 [1918].

Vieyra, Daniel I. "The Architecture of America's Roadside Lodging from Its Beginning to the Interstate Era." Unpublished Ph.D. dissertation. Cleveland: Case Western Reserve University, 1995.

Warner, W. Lloyd, with Marchia Meeker and Kenneth Eells. *Social Class in America: A Manual of Procedure for the Measurement of Social Status*. New York: Harper & Row, 1949.

Whyte, William H. *The Organization Man.* Garden City, N.Y.: Doubleday Anchor Books, 1956.

Wilson, Alexander. *The Culture of Nature: North American Landscape from Disney to the Exxon Valdez.* Toronto: Between the Lines, 1991.

Wolfe, Tom. *The Kandy-Kolored Tangerine-Flake Streamline Baby.* New York: Farrar, Straus and Giroux (Noonday Press), 1966.

Wolff, Janet. "On the Road Again: Metaphors of Travel in Cultural Criticism." *Cultural Studies* 7,2 (1993): 224–39.

Wrong, Dennis. "The Oversocialized Conception of Man in Sociology." *American Sociological Review* 26 (1961): 183–93.

Index

accountability 3, 104
adventure 118
advertising 10, 29, 31, 37–38, 46, 54
African-Americans, cars and 45–48, 50
Allen, Woody: *Annie Hall* 120
amateurism 13, 32, 38
American Medical Association 101–2
American Tailgater 82, 84
AMT Models 52
L'Année sociologique 117
Apprentice, The 126–27
architecture 10, 21, 34, 38, 43–44, 63, 117, 119–20
Arendt, Hannah: *The Human Condition* 21
Aspen Design Conference 121
audiovisual instruction 123
authority 54, 108
auto-camping 43
auto courts 44
automobility 9, 13–14, 41, 44; democracy and 45–50; football and 50, 70; freedom and 45–50; *see also* cars
autonomous individuality 9, 13, 41
autonomy, university 3

baby boomers 115
Balsley, Gene 11, 50–51, 54
Bank of America 25, 28
barbecuing 81–86, 95
Barris, George 51, 53
basketball 103
Beastie Boys 6
Bellah, Robert: *Habits of the Heart* 79
Bethlehem Steel 25

Beverly Hillbillies 126
"Big Three" automakers 30, 32, 81
Blevins, John 103
Boeckmann, Bert 82
Boorstin, Daniel J. 43–44
Boston Tea Party 6
Bourdieu, Pierre 38
Bowl season 57
Bradsher, Keith: *High and Mighty* 80
Brand, Myles 100–101, 103
branding, *see* corporate branding
Bretton Woods Conference 25, 28
Brewer, Bill "Dog," 78
Brewer, Charlie 136n9
Brinkmann Corporation 82
Bruneau, William 104
bureaucratized professionalism 108
Bush, George W. 57
business, football and 59–61, 81–86; higher education and 97

Cahn, Joe 85
Camp, Walter 60–61, 63, 86
capitalism 13, 54, 79, 81–86
cars 8–9, 11, 32, 33–34, 41–55, 80, 120; African-Americans and 45–48, 50; motels and 43–45; ownership of 44–45; women and 45, 48–50; *see also* automobility
Carvey, Dana 5
centralization 2, 31–32, 59
cheerleaders 50
Chow, Jason 82
class 20, 25, 27, 29, 32–33, 41, 46, 79, 94–95
class aristocracy 98
class-consciousness 14, 79, 86–87
class homogeneity 88
classical curriculum 116
classical studies 107

class identification 32
classism 36
class mobility 14, 79
class solidarity 14
class stability 88
Coca-Cola 30
Cohen, David K. 106
college football, *see* football
Columbia University 90, 92
comic strips 29, 33, 53
communication 117
community 43, 103; sociability and 2; tailgating and 77–81
community togetherness 14
"computerized zone," 123
computers, education and 123–25, 130
conformism/conformity 2, 15, 46, 77–81
consumer capitalism, market-driven 13, 15–16, 30, 41
consumer conformity, hot-rodders and 50–55
consumerism 104–9
corporate branding 15, 98, 101, 107
corporate capitalism 79, 81–86
corporate growth 14
corporate restraint 32
corporatization 36, 45–46, 58
Coughlin, Father 134n19
counterculture 5–6, 37
Cox, Sidney 26
Crane, Stephen 67
Crash 46–47
cultural capital 32, 38
cultural studies 1, 10, 19–40
cultural violence 13
curriculum: classical 116; standardized 16

Dallas 127
Dartmouth College 79, 87–95
Davis, Richard Harding 67
decentralization 34
deconstruction 38
decontextualization 123–24
Deland, Loren 136n9
DeLillo, Don: *End Zone* 64–65

democracy 34, 38, 41, 120; automobility and 45–50
democratic possibility 34
democratization 13
Denney, Harmer 21
Denney, Katherine 22
Denney, Randall 28
Denney, Reuel 2–4, 9–13, 15–16, 88, 98, 123, 127, 131–32; adulthood of 25–28; "American Youth Today," 13; *The Astonished Muse* 9–11, 13, 20, 26, 30, 33, 69; childhood of 21–25; *The Connecticut River* 28; consumerism and 104–5; cultural studies and 29–34; distance education and 124–25; football and 58–59, 62, 69–70; higher education and 107–10; hot-rodders and 50–54; "The Leisure Society," 30, 95; *The Lonely Crowd*, *see under* Riesman; postmodernism of 37–40; sociability, technology, learning and 117–20, 124–25; sociology of 19–40; "The Suppliant Skyscrapers," 119; tailgating and 78, 81, 86–88; television and 121, 126, 130–31; vocationalism and 115–16, 130; youth and sociability and 98, 104, 113, 115–16
de Tocqueville, Alexis 33; *Democracy in America* 20
Detroit 30, 32, 44, 51–52
Dewey, John 125
discrimination 69
dissent, meaningful 105
distance education 15–16, 115–32
do-it-yourselfers 29–30, 46, 80–81, 106
Dorais, Gus 59
Dragnet 126
drinking, student 102–3, 111–12
Durkheim, Emile 117

EA Sports 112
"edutainment," 1, 112–13; classroom as 98–103; popular culture and 128–32

Index • 149

Eliot, T.S. 33
Ellis of Rugby 32
Emerson, Ralph Waldo 45
entertainment, business of 38, 45–46; sport as 66–70; 98–103
ER 126
ethnicity 33, 41, 46, 69, 79, 86, 98–99
"Everything Bad Is Good For You" thesis 125–28

Farrar, Eleanor 106
Fear Factor 126
Federal Communication Corporation Hearings 121
feminization 46
folkways, industrial 31, 60
football 2, 8–11, 13, 14, 21, 30–32, 34, 57–70, 104; as entertainment 98–103; as national spectacle 66–70; as social narrative 68–70; automobility and 50, 70; British, *see* soccer; business and 59–61, 81–86; female exclusion and 69; industrial America and 58–61; rules of 58–61; tailgating and 71–95; technology and 61–66, 69
Ford, Bill 80
Ford, Henry 14, 47, 59
Foucault, Michel 45
Frederick, Charles R., Jr. 8, 77–79, 85, 95
freedom 41, 43; automobility and 45–50; *see also* autonomous individuality
Freeman, Richard B. 109–10
Frisby, David 117, 119
Fund for the Advancement of Education 122
funding, university 3

Gale Group 81
Galpin Motors 82
GameCube 112
gambling 110–11, 118
gaming 16, 125–28, 129
"Gasoline Alley," 33, 53
Gatto, John Taylor 107

gender 33, 41, 46, 48–50, 79, 94–95, 102
Giannini, A.P. 25
Gillette, Felix 112
Gilroy, Paul 47–48
Glazer, Nathan 9, 28; *The Lonely Crowd, see under* Riesman
global village 123
Goldman, Emma 7
golf 30
Goodman, Paul 109
Grove, The (University of Mississippi) 77–79, 85, 88, 93–95

Handlin, Oscar: *The Uprooted* 20–21
Harvard University 8, 58, 136n9
Hearst, William Randolph: *Journal* 67
Hearth, Patio & Barbecue Association (HPBA) 81, 83–84
Heath, Joseph: *Rebel Sell*, 5–6, 37, 80
higher education: as style for life 109–13; branding of 101, 107; computers and 123–25; consumerism and 104–9; gambling and 110–11; parties and 97–113; television and 121–23, 125–28; training vs. 108–9, 116
highways, construction of 44
Hinkey, Frank 136n9
Hoffer, Eric: *The True Believer* 21
holidaying 43–45
Hollingshead, August B.: *Elmtown's Youth* 19
Home Depot 81
homogeneity 1, 13, 88, 105
homogenization 1, 2, 15
hotels 44
hot-rodding 2, 10–11, 13, 21, 30, 32, 78; consumer conformity and 50–55
Hot Rod magazine 52–53
Hsu, Francis L.K.: *Clan, Case and Club* 20

identity: formation of 38; politics of 3

I Love Lucy 126
Indiana University 103
individualism 45, 118; rugged 24, 118
individuality 32, 46–47; see also autonomous individuality
industrial folkways 31, 60
inner-direction 11–12, 29, 77
Intercollegiate Football Association 58
intercollegiate sports 15, 58
Internet 127, 131
Ivy League 90–92

Johnson, Jack 47
Johnson, Steven 112, 125–28, 130; *Everything Bad Is Good For You* 125
Judd, Ron 93–94

Kasdan, Lawrence: *The Big Chill* 77
Kerouac, Jack 47; *On the Road* 45
Knight, Phil 65
knowledge: construction of 124; packaging of 15, 123

Lakehead University 84–85
learning outputs 123
learning "packages," 123
Leary, Timothy 35
leisure 23, 29, 117
leisure class 20
Lévi-Strauss, Claude: *Structural Anthropology* 21
Lewis, Corinne Keller 119
liberal education 116
life-long learning 115–16
Livingstone, D.W. 110
Lombardi, Vince 85
Lonely Crowd 12–15, 46, 77–81, 95, 98, 128–32; consumerism vs. 104–9; see also Riesman
Lost 127
Lower, Arthur: *Canadians in the Making* 43
Lynes, Russell: *The Tastemakers* 20
"lyric sport," decline of 57–70

machine mentality 123
machine reality 123
Madden, John 112
Marcuse, Herbert 45
Marx, Karl 117
mass media 3, 10, 20, 21, 29, 33–34, 46, 54, 120, 124, 131; postmodernism and 37–38
Matson, Floyd W.: *The Broken Image* 20
Maxwell, Bob 61–62
McDonald's 42
McGill University 58
"McLearning," 15
McLuhan, Eric 120
McLuhan, Marshall 16, 33, 54, 119–20, 121, 123–24, 126–27, 131; *The Mechanical Bride* 33, 121; *Understanding Media* 20, 33
McMaster University 128–29
media, see mass media
medium as message/massage 33, 120
Meredith, Don 110
militarization 13, 36
Miller, Tony 81
Mills, C. Wright 80
Mississippi, University of (Ole Miss) 77, 85, 88, 94
Mississippi State University 65–66
mobility: individual 43, 45; social 32, 41, 69, 86
Montana, University of 71–76
motels 43–45; architecture of 44
motor courts 44
"motorscape," 44
Myers, Mike 5

National Collegiate Athletic Association (NCAA) 86–87, 99–100
National Hot Rod Association 53
National Lampoon's Animal House 10
newspapers, football coverage in 67–69
Nicolson, Sir Harold: *Good Behaviour* 20
Niedzviecki, Hal 45–46, 80, 90

Nike 65–66
Noble, David 108–9
normalization 32
Norton, Ruth Lois 27
Notre Dame University 59

O.C., The 111–13
Oldenburg, Ray 97, 103, 110, 113; *The Great Good Place* 97
Oldfield, Barney 47
Ole Miss, *see* University of Mississippi
O'Neil, P.J. 82
Oregon, University of 65–66, 71–76, 87–88, 91–92, 99–101, 103
Oregonian 68–69
Oriard, Michael 58, 60, 67–69
other-direction 12, 15, 29, 46, 77, 80, 103
overconformity 77
overqualification 110
overskill 109–10

Pacific-10 Conference (Pac-10) 72, 75, 100
"participative purists," 78–79
party/partying 5–17, 98–103, 104, 109, 113, 128, 130; *see also* tailgating
Pennsylvania, University of 58
Pennsylvania State University 103
Pitt-Rivers, J.A.: *The People of the Sierra* 20
play 117; Americans at 29–35; intersection with education 2; intersection with work 2, 21, 30–31, 38, 95
Playboy 101
play-by-play commentary 68
play impulse 16
PlayStation3, 16–17, 112
popular culture 1, 38, 121, 125; edutainment and 128–32
Postman, Neil: *The Disappearance of Childhood* 105
postmodernism 10, 37–40
Potter, Andrew: *Rebel Sell*: *see under* Heath

Pound, Ezra 33
Powell, Arthur G. 106
Price Is Right, The 127
Princeton Review 101, 104
Princeton University 58
professionalism 13, 15, 32, 38; bureaucratized 108
professionalization 30–32
protest demonstrations 36–37
Pulitzer, Joseph: *World* 67
Putnam, Robert 79

racism 36, 46–48
radio 33
Radio Corporation of America (RCA) 122
Ramsey, Alice Huyler 49
reality television 125–27
"rear-view mirror," 120, 123
Rebel Walk 77–78
Register-Guard (Eugene) 83–84
repressive tolerance 45
Revel 52
Reynolds, Malvina: "Little Boxes," 77, 105
Riesman, David 27–28, 31–32, 98; *The Lonely Crowd* 9, 11, 15, 20, 33, 77, 80, 131
Rockne, Knute 14, 31–32, 59
Rolling Stones 6
Roosevelt, Theodore 61–62
Rose Bowl 100–101
Roth, Ed 51, 53–54
rugby 14, 31–32
Rutgers University 58

Salano, Reuel 21
Saturday Night Live 5
Sayles, John: *Return of the Secaucus 7* 77
Schmidt, Jeff 108; *Disciplined Minds* 108
scholarships, athletic 87
Schudson, Michael 67
Schuller, Reverend Robert 42
Schwartz, Eugene S. 109
scientific football 61–66
Scopes Monkey Trial 25

Seiler, Cotton 41, 45
Seinfeld 126
self-determination 9, 45
Sevilla, Universidad de 103
Shaw, Gary 65
Sherrill, Jackie 66
Simmel, Georg 16, 21, 117–19, 123, 127, 131; "The Adventure," 118; "The Alpine Journey," 117–18; "Bridge and Door," 119; "The Sociology of Sociability," 118
Simmel, Gertrud 117
Simpsons, The 126
"Smilin' Jack," 53
Smith, Al 25
soccer 14, 31–32, 98
soccer moms 50
sociability 14–16, 70, 79, 85, 87, 97–98, 103, 106–7, 113; community and 2; democratized 116; distance education and 115–32; scholarship and 127; technology, learning and 117–20, 123; youth and 98
social control 108
social democracy 25
socialization 2
social mobility 32, 41, 69, 86
social movements 36–37
social narrative, football as 68–70
social-network complexity 127
sociation 117
sociology 1960s and 35–37; objective 37
Sopranos, The 126
space 41
special access programs 3
spectatorship 31
Sperber, Murray 99, 101, 110, 113
sports history 13; as social progress 86
sports recruitment 99
sportscasters 64
sportswriters 14; football and 66–70
Spragens, Thomas A. 122
standardization 31, 32, 59, 108
Starsky and Hutch 126
Stephens College 121

student activism 36–37
subcultures 2, 29, 38
suburbanization 42–43
Suellentrop, Chris 112
Super Bowl 77, 110
Survivor 126–27
SUVs 80, 82, 85

tailgating 7–9, 11, 14–15, 33, 71–95, 98, 102–3, 106–7, 110
Taylor, Frederick Winslow 86
technology 3; football and 61–66, 69; schools and 120, 121–28, 131–32; sociability, learning and 117–20
television 10, 33–34, 120, 124, 125–28, 129–31; learning and 121–23; reality 125–27
tennis 30
Texas, University of 101
"third place," *see* Oldenburg
Three's Company 126–27
togetherness 77–81
tourist courts 44
tradition-directed 77
Trafford, Bernie 136n9
training, education vs. 108–9, 116
transportation 117
Trump, Donald 126–27
24 [TV show] 127
Twitchell, James, B. 15, 48, 104–5

"unfreedom," 45
university: as experience 14, 97–98; as place 14, 97–98; consumerist model of training at 104–9; in 1960s 35–37; *see also* higher education
urban spaces 38

vacations, *see* holidaying
Veblen, Thorstein 20, 33, 98; *The Higher Learning in America* 98; "vicarious we," 31
video games 125–28
Vieyra, Daniel I. 41–43, 135n2
violence: cultural 13; football and 63–65

Index • 153

virtual reality 124
vocationalism 115–16, 130
volunteering 116

Warner, W. Lloyd: *Social Class in America* 20
Washington, University of 93
Wayne's World 5
WebCT 129
Weber, Max 54–55, 117
Wheel of Fortune 127
Whitman, Walt 45
Whyte, William H.: *The Organization Man* 77
Wilson, Alexander 42

Wolfe, Tom 51, 53–54
women: cars and 45, 48–50; football and 69; tailgating and 94–95
Woodstock 77
work 117; intersection with play 2, 21, 30–31, 38, 95

Xbox 112

Yale University 8, 58, 60, 63, 86, 107, 136n9
youth 98, 104–5, 113, 115–16

Zingrone, Frank 120